DIRECTORY OF BRITISH GEOLOGICAL MUSEUMS

Cover illustration: The dinosaur *Cetiosaurus* on display at the Leicestershire Museum and Art Gallery, courtesy of Leicestershire Museums. Photograph by Steve Thursfield.

DIRECTORY OF BRITISH GEOLOGICAL MUSEUMS

Geological Society Miscellaneous Paper No.18

Compiled and edited by John R. Nudds

on behalf of the Geological Curators' Group

Published by The Geological Society on behalf of the Geological Curators' Group 1994

The Geological Society

The Society was founded in 1807 as the Geological Society of London and is the oldest geological society in the world. It received its Royal Charter in 1825 for the purpose of 'investigating the mineral structure of the Earth'. The Society is Britain's national society for geology with a membership of 7,500 (1993). It has countrywide coverage and approximately 1,000 members reside overseas. The Society is responsible for all aspects of the geological sciences including professional matters. The Society has its own publishing house, which produces the Society's international journals, books and maps, and which acts as the European distributor for publications of the American Association of Petroleum Geologists and the Geological Society of America.

Fellowship is open to those holding a recognized honours degree in geology or cognate subject and who have at least two years' relevant postgraduate experience, or who have not less than six years' relevant experience in geology or a cognate subject. A Fellow who has not less than five years' relevant postgraduate experience in the practice of geology may apply for validation and, subject to approval, may be able to use the designatory letters C Geol (Chartered Geologist).

Further information about the Society is available from the Membership Manager, The Geological Society, Burlington House, Piccadilly, London W1V 0JU, UK.

The Geological Curators' Group (Registered Charity No. 296050 is affiliated to The Geological Society of London.

Published by The Geological Society from:
The Geological Society Publishing House
Unit 7
Brassmill Enterprise Centre
Brassmill Lane
Bath BA1 3JN
UK
(*Orders:* Tel 0225 445046
Fax 0225 442836)

Registered Charity No. 210161

First published 1994

The publisher makes no representation, express or implied, with regard to the accuracy of the information contained in this book and cannot accept any legal responsibility for any errors or omissions that may be made.

© The Geological Society 1994. All rights reserved. No reproduction, copy or transmission of this publication may be made without written permission. No paragraph of this publication may be reproduced, copied or transmitted save with the provisions of the Copyright Licensing Agency, 90 Tottenham Court Road, London W1P 9HE. Users registered with the Copyright Clearance Center, 27 Congress Street, Salem, MA 01970, USA: the item fee code for this publication is 0305-0394/94/$07.00.

British Library Cataloguing in Publication Data
A catalogue record for this book is available from the British Library
ISBN 1-897799-08-X

Distributors
USA
AAPG Bookstore
PO Box 979
Tulsa
OK 74101-0979
USA
(*Orders:* Tel (918) 584-2555
Fax (918) 548-0469)

Australia
Australian Mineral Foundation
63 Conyngham Street
Glenside
South Australia 5065
Australia
(*Orders:* Tel (08) 379-0444
Fax (08) 379-4634)

India
Affiliated East-West Press PVT Ltd
G-1/16 Ansari Road
New Delhi 110 002
India
(*Orders:* Tel (11) 327-9113
Fax (11) 326-0538)

Japan
Kanda Book Trading Co.
Tanikawa Building
3-2 Kanda Surugadai
Chiyoda-Ku
Tokyo 101
Japan
(*Orders:* Tel (03) 3255-3497
Fax (03) 3255-3495)

Typeset and printed by City Print (MK) Ltd,
Milton Keynes MK3 7QT, UK

Contents

Preface	vii
Introduction	viii

SCOTLAND

Dumfries	
Dumfries Museum	1
Dundee	
Dundee Art Galleries and Museums	2
Edinburgh	
Royal Museum of Scotland	3
Glasgow	
Glasgow Art Gallery and Museum	6
Hunterian Museum	8
Inverness	
Inverness Museum and Art Gallery	10
Montrose	
Montrose Museum	11
Nairn	
Nairn Literary Institute Museum	12
Perth	
Perth Museum and Art Gallery	13

WALES

Cardiff	
National Museum of Wales	14

NORTHERN IRELAND

Belfast	
Ulster Museum	17

REPUBLIC OF IRELAND

Cork	
Cork Geological Museum	20
Dublin	
National Museum of Ireland	22
Trinity College Geological Museum	23
Galway	
James Mitchell Museum	26

NORTH AND NORTH-WEST ENGLAND

Bolton	
Bolton Museum and Art Gallery	28
Carlisle	
Tullie House Museum and Art Gallery	29
Clitheroe	
Clitheroe Castle Museum	30
Kendal	
Kendal Museum	32
Liverpool	
Liverpool Museum	34
Manchester	
The Manchester Museum	37
Middlesbrough	
Cleveland County Museum Service	40
Newcastle-upon-Tyne	
The Hancock Museum	41
Sunderland	
Sunderland Museum and Art Gallery	43
Warrington	
Warrington Museum and Art Gallery	44
Wigan	
Wigan and Leigh College Geology and Mining Museum	45

YORKSHIRE AND HUMBERSIDE

Doncaster	
Doncaster Museum and Art Gallery	47
Huddersfield	
Tolson Memorial Museum	48
Keighley	
Cliffe Castle Museum	49
Kingston Upon Hull	
Kingston Upon Hull Museums and Art Galleries	50
Leeds	
Leeds City Museum	52
Scunthorpe	
Scunthorpe Museum and Art Gallery	53
Sheffield	
Sheffield City Museum	54
Skipton	
Craven Museum	56
Whitby	
Whitby Museum	57
York	
Yorkshire Museum	58

MIDLANDS

Birmingham	
Birmingham Museum and Art Gallery	60
Buxton	
Buxton Museum and Art Gallery	61
Derby	
Derby City Museum and Art Gallery	62
Dudley	
Dudley Museum and Art Gallery	64
Hereford	
Hereford City Museum	67
Leicester	
Leicestershire Museums, Arts and Records Service	68
Ludlow	
Ludlow Museum	69
Nottingham	
British Geological Survey	71
Nottingham Natural History Museum	75
Shrewsbury	
Rowley's House	77

Stoke-on-Trent
   Stoke-on-Trent City Museum and
     Art Gallery   79
Telford
   Jackfield Tile Museum   80
Warwick
   Warwickshire Museum   81
Wolverhampton
   Wolverhampton Art Gallery and Museum   82
Worcester
   Worcester City Museum and Art Gallery   83

EAST–CENTRAL AND SOUTH–EAST ENGLAND
Aylesbury
   Buckinghamshire County Museum   84
Brighton
   The Booth Museum of Natural History   86
Cambridge
   Sedgwick Museum   88
Colchester
   Colchester Museums   90
Dartford
   Dartford Borough Museum   91
Haslemere
   Haslemere Educational Museum   92
Hitchin
   North Hertfordshire Museums   94
Ipswich
   Ipswich Museum   95
London
   Horniman Public Museum   96
   Natural History Museum: Department of Mineralogy   97
   Natural History Museum: Department of Palaeontology   101
   Passmore Edwards Museum   104
Northampton
   Northampton Central Museum and Art Gallery   105
Norwich
   Norwich Castle Museum   107
Oxford
   Oxford University Museum   108
Peterborough
   Peterborough City Museum and Art Gallery   110
Portsmouth
   Portsmouth Natural Science Museum and Aquarium   111

Reading
   Reading Museums Service   112
Saffron Walden
   Saffron Walden Museum   113
St Albans
   Museum of St Albans   114
Sandown
   Museum of Isle of Wight Geology   115
Winchester
   Hampshire County Council Museums Service   116
Wisbech
   Wisbech and Fenland Museum   117

WEST–CENTRAL AND SOUTH–WEST ENGLAND
Bristol
   Bristol City Museum and Art Gallery   119
Devizes
   Devizes Museum   121
Dorchester
   Dorset County Museum   122
Exeter
   Royal Albert Memorial Museum   123
Lyme Regis
   Lyme Regis (Philpot) Museum   125
Plymouth
   Plymouth City Museum and Art Gallery   127
Redruth
   Camborne School of Mines Geological Museum   128
Taunton
   Somerset County Museum   130
Torquay
   Torquay Museum   132
Truro
   Royal Cornwall Museum   133
Wells
   Wells Museum   134
Weston-super-Mare
   Woodspring Museum   135

CHANNEL ISLANDS
Guernsey
   Guernsey Museum and Art Gallery   136
Jersey
   La Hougue Bie Museum   138

Appendix   139

Preface

This directory is the result of a survey undertaken by the Geological Curators' Group between 1991 and 1993 by the Groups' Recorder, Dr John R. Nudds, Keeper of Geology at The Manchester Museum, University of Manchester. The initial survey included all those museums listed as providing a geological service in the *Rocks Fossils and Minerals Guide* published by the Geological Curators' Group. It has subsequently been extended to include some additional United Kingdom museums and the major museums in the Irish Republic and the Channel Islands. Inclusion in the Directory does not depend solely on the size of the collections, but also takes into account their importance and the presence or absence of geologically qualified curatorial staff. Only public collections are included; university collections are only listed in those cases where there is also a public museum attached.

The museums are herein divided into geographical regions within which they are listed alphabetically according to place names. An appendix lists additional museums with geological collections which are not included in the main text.

Introduction

The Geological Curators' Group (GCG) was formed in 1974 to improve the state and status of geology in museums. The Group aims to improve access to and knowledge of geological collections for all purposes - from leisure and tourism to education and science. The GCG has rightly acquired a reputation in the museum world for pushing forward the boundaries of professionalism among its members, both personal and institutional. Each Chairman has left his mark (and I look forward to the time when we can add a feminine possessive pronoun) in this respect and each new incumbent needs to consider their own three year chairmanship and what it might achieve. In my own case, I had become somewhat frustrated that as a practising curator, access to information about fellow institutions and curators was not always easy. A great deal of information has been accumulated which concerns collections but this has generally only been available in specialist literature and was never accompanied by other useful information such as the location of the museum or its telephone number. Similarly, members of the burgeoning amateur geological and mineralogical societies in the country have often requested sources of information about geological museums in areas of the country which they were due to visit. This situation was improved by the splendid *Geologists' Directory* published by the Geological Society in which museums with geological collections were listed . This, however, was a publication aimed at the professional geologist and not the lay public, and gave no information about geological services or collections. Bearing all of this in mind, I was therefore determined that one result of my chairmanship of the GCG would be a publication which brought together a list of geological museums in the country, details of their collections and geological services as well as opening hours, location etc. I was fortunate in being presented with a committee to Chair which already boasted the post of Recorder, occupied by Dr John Nudds, whose brief it was to be variously involved with information about museums, collections and curators. I was perhaps even more fortunate that my suggestion for this Directory was embraced with all of the enthusiasm and vigour which have been hallmarks of so much of what the GCG has been involved with in the past. The result of this personal and group commitment lies within these pages and I am very grateful to John Nudds for his hard, careful and persistent work in drawing this information together. I must also thank Nigel Cunningham, our Brighton-based designer, for his help with the look of the final product, and Mike Collins and his staff at the Geological Society Publishing House for their important role in the Directory's birth. Finally, I must thank all of the participating museums who responded well to the original survey and later prompting.

John Cooper

Booth Museum of Natural History, Brighton

Chairman, Geological Curators' Group 1990-1992

SCOTLAND
DUMFRIES
Dumfries Museum

Address:
The Observatory, Dumfries, DG2 7SW. Telephone 0387 53374.

Administration:
Nithsdale District Council.

Admission:
Free.

Times of opening:
Monday - Saturday 10.00 - 13.00, 14.00 - 17.00, Sunday 14.00 - 17.00. Closed Sunday and Monday October to March.

History:

Dumfries Museum was founded in 1835 as an astronomical observatory and museum in the eighteenth century stone windmill at the top of Corberry Hill. A camera obscura was installed in the following summer and the building was opened to the public on 1st August 1836. The tower rooms were furnished with show cases in 1842 and the main hall was added in 1862 to house the collections of the newly formed Dumfriesshire and Galloway Natural History and Antiquarian Society. The Museum was taken over by the Town Council of the Royal Burgh of Dumfries in 1934 and after local government reorganisation in 1975 came under the jurisdiction of Nithsdale District Council.

Principal collections:

Grierson Collection - minerals of Wanlockhead/Leadhills area.

Major strengths:

Fossil reptile footprints from Permian sandstone.

Number of specimens:

c.5,000.

Published catalogues:

McCracken, A. 1964. The geological collections of the museum. Transactions of the Dumfries and Galloway Natural History and Antiquarian Society **41**, 9.

Truckell, A.E. 1966. The Grierson Collection, Thornhill and its dispersal. Ibid., **43**, 63.

Williams, J. 1964. The mineralogical collections of Dumfries Burgh Museum. Ibid., **41**, 201.

Williams, J. 1965. Further notes on mineralogy in Dumfries and Galloway. Ibid., **42**, 14.

Displays:

Fossil reptile footprints in Permian sandstone; other fossils; structural rocks; minerals; metals and mining; coal mining and stone quarrying.

Research facilities:

Museum Library.

Staff:

Museum Officer, Siobhan Ratchford.

Compiler:

S. Ratchford.

SCOTLAND
DUNDEE
Dundee Art Galleries and Museums

Address:
McManus Galleries, Albert Square, Dundee DD1 1DA.
Telephone 0382 23141; Fax 0382 27621.

Administration:
City of Dundee District Council.

Admission:
Free.

Times of opening:
Monday - Saturday 10.00 - 17.00.

History:
Museum collections were begun in 1870 based on the remaining specimens of the Watt Institute Collections. Few of these appear to have been geological. Professional staff were first employed in the museum in about 1947, but expansion to the current level of staffing did not occur until the early 1960's. There are now 5 natural sciences staff, 2 of whom are technicians. Geological collections were housed in the McManus Galleries until the late 1970's when they were transferred to Barrack Street Museum (250 metres W of main building) during a major rationalisation of collections.

Principal collections:
The Kinnaird Collection (including Old Red Sandstone fish)) is probably the most noteworthy, although most of the figured/referred material is in the Royal Museum of Scotland.

Major strengths:
Old Red Sandstone fossils.

Number of specimens:
c.5,000.

Displays:
Several on local geology incorporated with other aspects of natural history.

Staff:
Assistant Keeper (Geology), David S. Henderson.

Other information:
Public enquiry service is operated. Specimen loans are available. NSGSD record centre.

Compiler:
David S. Henderson.

SCOTLAND
EDINBURGH
Royal Museum of Scotland

Address:
Chambers Street, Edinburgh EH1 1JF. Telephone 031 225 7534; Fax 031 220 4819.

Administration:
National Museums of Scotland.

Admission:
Free.

Times of opening:
Monday - Saturday 10.00 - 17.00, Sunday 14.00 - 17.00. Closed December 25,26, January 1,2.

History:

The National Museums of Scotland were brought into being in 1985 when the National Museum of Antiquities of Scotland and the Royal Scottish Museum, with several smaller museums, were merged by Act of Parliament. The former Royal Scottish Museum, now the Royal Museum of Scotland (Chambers Street), houses collections of Natural History, Geology, Decorative Arts of the World and Science, Technology and Working Life, and can be traced back through various changes of name to the foundation of the first National Museum for Scotland in 1854, established under the name of the Industrial Museum of Scotland.

At that time, this Museum inherited the contents of the old College Museum of Edinburgh University, which incorporated the remains of several even earlier collections (e.g. Robert Sibbald, Andrew Balfour, John Walker, James Hutton) although few specimens from these can now be identified. Robert Jameson had assiduously built up the College Museum collections between 1804 and 1854, and his major interest was geology, then in its infancy. Jameson left a very rich nucleus for the future Geology Department: he encouraged his students to collect world-wide, and his association with Louis Agassiz led to the acquisition of many specimens which became the latter's types.

From 1875 to 1906 the collections were in the care of the eminent vertebrate palaeontologist, Dr R.H. Traquair, who studied and described many new forms, made a notable collection himself and acquired numerous large collec-

The Main Hall

tions in all branches of geology. The Geology Department continues to pursue active policies of collecting and research, specialising particularly in fossil arthropods and fishes, mineral identification and the history of geology.

Principal collections:

Joseph Blair - Carboniferous vertebrates (1857); Robert Dunlop - Carboniferous fossils (1957); Free Church College - John Fleming's fossils (1966); Lady Gordon Cumming - Old Red Sandstone fishes (1973); William Gubbin - general fossils (1911); D. Hardie - crinoids and arthropods (1897); J. Henderson - crinoids and arthropods (1885); Sir William Jardine - footprints (1875); Archie Lamont - Pentland Hills fossils (1976); Albert Long - Carboniferous plants (1962); Hugh Miller - general fossils (1859); James Neilson - Carboniferous fossils (1911); H.A. Nicholson - corals (1879); Charles Peach - general fossils (1875); James Powrie - Old Red Sandstone fossils (1891); Royal Society of Edinburgh - general fossils (1878); Stan Wood - Carboniferous vertebrates (1971); James Wright - Crinoids (1958); Marquis of Breadalbane - minerals (1981); Patrick Dudgeon - minerals (1890); Matthew Forster

Heddle - minerals (1894); Robert Miln - agates (1907); A.M. Cockburn - St Kilda rocks; Commissioners of the Great Exhibition - rocks (1851); Highland & Agricultural Society - rocks (1859); HM Geological Survey of Scotland - rocks, geological maps and models (1899); Charles Maclaren - rocks (1866).

Major strengths:

The significant collections listed above ensure that the following areas are very well represented: Scottish Carboniferous palaeontology; ore minerals from the last century heyday of the Leadhills mining industry, SW Scotland; agates and related gems from various parts of Scotland. Other areas of strength have also built up steadily over the years: fossil plants, crinoids, eurypterids (water scorpions), Palaeozoic fishes and land vertebrates (early amphibians and the earliest reptile). Although much of the reference material illustrates the geology of Scotland, there is also an extensive range of foreign specimens for comparison. Copies of the department's collecting policy are available on request.

Number of specimens:

c.110,000 fossils (80,000 invertebrates, 10,000 plants, 20,000 vertebrates), c.60,000 minerals (15,000 Scottish, 45,000 General), c.20,000 rocks; 1148 type specimens, 3383 figured specimens.

Published catalogues:

The following catalogues have all appeared in the *Royal Scottish Museum Information Series: Geology:*

No.1   Henrichsen, I.G.C. 1970. A catalogue of fossil vertebrates in the Royal Scottish Museum, Edinburgh. Part 1 Actinopterygii.

No.2   Henrichsen, I.G.C. 1971. A catalogue of fossil vertebrates in the Royal Scottish Museum, Edinburgh. Part 2 Agnatha.

No.3   Henrichsen, I.G.C. 1972. A catalogue of fossil vertebrates in the Royal Scottish Museum, Edinburgh. Part 3 Actinistia and Dipnoi.

No.4   Sime, I.F. 1972. A catalogue of Carboniferous corals in the Royal Scottish Museum, Edinburgh.

No.5   Paton, R.L. 1975. A catalogue of fossil vertebrates in the Royal Scottish Museum, Edinburgh. Part 4 Amphibia and Reptilia.

No.6   Paton, R.L. 1976. A catalogue of fossil vertebrates in the Royal Scottish Museum, Edinburgh. Part 5 Acanthodii.

No.7   Benton, M.J. 1979. H.A. Nicholson, invertebrate palaeontologist: bibliography and catalogue of his type and figured material.

No.8   Baird, W.J. 1980. A catalogue of trilobites in the Royal Scottish Museum, Edinburgh.

No.9   Paton, R.L. 1981. A catalogue of fossil vertebrates in the Royal Scottish Museum, Edinburgh. Part 6 Placodermi.

No.10   Sutherland, A.G. 1990. A catalogue of Carboniferous corals in the Royal Museum of Scotland, Edinburgh.

The following publications also catalogue Royal Museum of Scotland material:

Andrews, S.M. 1982. *The discovery of fossil fishes in Scotland up to 1845, with checklists of Agassiz's figured specimens.* Royal Scottish Museum Studies, Edinburgh.

Macpherson, H.G. and Livingstone, A. 1982. Glossary of Scottish mineral species 1981. *Scottish Journal of Geology,* **18**, 5-47.

Livingstone, A. and Macpherson, H.G. 1983. Fifth supplementary list of British minerals (Scottish). *Mineralogical Magazine,* **47**, 99-105.

Stace, H.E., Pettitt, C.W.A. and Waterston, C.D. 1987. *Natural Science Collections in Scotland.* National Museums of Scotland, Edinburgh.

Other publications:

Evolution: general booklet on the permanent exhibition in the Royal Scottish Museum. Royal Scottish Museum, Edinburgh, 1975.

Evolution 3: The Age of Reptiles (The Mesozoic Era). Royal Scottish Museum, Edinburgh, 1977.

Baird, W.J. 1991 (3rd edition). *The scenery of Scotland.* National Museums of Scotland, Edinburgh.

Chaloner, W.G. and Macdonald, P. 1980. *Plants invade the land.* HMSO.

Macpherson, H.G. 1989. Agates. British Museum (Natural History), London and National Museums of Scotland, Edinburgh.

Calder, J. (Ed.) 1989. The wealth of a nation in the National Museums of Scotland. National Museums of Scotland, Edinburgh and Richard Drew, Glasgow.

Calder, J. (Ed.) 1990. Royal Museum of Scotland Souvenir Booklet. National Museums of Scotland, Edinburgh.

Displays:

Geological displays are displayed in two main areas of the museum:

The North East Wing.

From the basement to the first floor, an exhibition on four levels is devoted to the fossil evidence for Evolution. The first level introduces the origin of life, while the others concentrate mainly on the story of backboned animals in the Palaeozoic (fishes and amphibians), Mesozoic (reptiles) and Cainozoic (mammals). These galleries are primarily for students, but are illustrated with numerous original fossils and reconstructions. Above this, on the second floor, the Mineral Hall introduces mineralogy, with sections on crystal colour and shape, fluorescence, gemstones and economically important minerals, including North Sea oil. There are fine mineral groups and meteorites from Scotland.

Other Second Floor Galleries.

Gallery 2-8 is being replanned and will house the new exhibition, *Sands of Time*. This will deal with Scotland's on-shore geology, relating it to oilfield geology off-shore. It will demonstrate the dynamic aspects of geology, and a collection of some 200 spectacular Scottish specimens will be on open display. The Fossils Gallery (2-10) is arranged systematically, from Protozoa through all major animal groups to vertebrates. Gallery 2-11 deals with fundamental geological processes, rock types and Scotland's mineral wealth. It also includes displays of Scottish agates, ornamental stones and building stones.

In addition, a new Museum of Scotland, in a new building to be opened in 1996 alongside the old one in Chambers Street, will include a major display, *Making the Landscape*, summarising the geological history of Scotland.

Staff:

Keeper of Geology, Dr W.D.I. Rolfe; Curators of Fossil Vertebrates, Dr M.A. Taylor, Dr R.L. Paton; Curator of Fossil Invertebrates and Plants, Mr W.J. Baird; Curators of Minerals, Dr A. Livingstone, Mr B. Jackson, Mr P.J. Davidson; Conservation Laboratory Manager, Mr R.J. Reekie; Conservator and Preparator, Mr C. Chaplin; Laboratory Assistant, Mrs S. Stevenson; Secretaries, Mrs S.D. Doddie, Mrs E. Rennie.

Other information:

As well as the permanent exhibits, the National Museums of Scotland offer a regular programme of lectures and gallery talks relevant to the collections, some of which are concerned with geology. Of particular interest are the geological walks and field trips for the non-specialist in the summer months. Behind the scenes visits to the Geological Laboratories can be arranged for parties.

Compiler:

S.M. Andrews

SCOTLAND
GLASGOW
Glasgow Art Gallery and Museum

Address:
Kelvingrove, Glasgow G3 8AG. Telephone 041 357 3929; Fax 041 357 4537.

Admission:
Free.

Times of opening:
Monday - Saturday 10.00 - 17.00, Sunday 11.00 - 17.00. Closed Christmas Day and New Year's Day.

History:

The museum collections were started in 1870. At this time they were housed in a converted mansion house in Kelvingrove Park while the present building, built for the International Exhibition, was opened as Glasgow Art Gallery and Museum in 1902. Geological material has been represented in the collections from the first year. The greatest growth took place during the 1890's and 1900's when the large collections of many prominent local geologists, members of the Geological Society of Glasgow, were acquired for the museum.

Principal collections:

Absalom, R.G. - Scottish Coal Measure plants; Alstone, J. - Red Crag fossils; Andersonian University or College, Glasgow - Miscellaneous fossils; Broom, R. - Tertiary mammal skulls and teeth from USA; Camp Siluria - Silurian fish and arthropods from Lesmahagow; Campbell, Lord A. - Tertiary plants from Ardtun, Mull; Coutts, J. - Scottish Quaternary fossils; Craig, R. - Carboniferous invertebrates from Ayrshire; Dairon, J. - Ordovician and Silurian graptolites from Southern Uplands; Fleming, Prof. J. - minerals, mainly Scottish; Geological Society of Glasgow - miscellaneous fossils; Glen, D.C. - world-wide minerals; Henderson, S.M.K. - rocks and thin sections mainly from Girvan; Hunter-Selkirk, J.R.S. - Scottish Carboniferous and Silurian fossils; Melven, W. - Devonian fish and Mesozoic fossils from north east Scotland; Pouillon-Williard, A. - French and German Mesozoic and Tertiary fossils; Pratt, A. -thin sections, mainly Scottish dolerites; Reid, J. - Devonian plants and fish; Robertson, D. - Scottish Quaternary fossils; Scott, A.C. - Carboniferous plants; Slimon, R. - Silurian eurypterids and phyllocarids from Lesmahagow; Thomson, J. - Scottish Carboniferous corals; Wood, S. - Carboniferous plants and amphibian from Bathgate; Young, J. - Scottish Carboniferous invertebrates.

Major strengths:

Rocks, minerals and fossils are represented in the geological collections. Fossils, mainly from Scotland, and in particular from the west of Scotland, form the largest and most important aspect. The main strengths within the palaeontological collections are Carboniferous invertebrates, Carboniferous plants, Silurian arthropods and fish, Ordovician and Silurian graptolites, Devonian fish and Quaternary invertebrates.

Number of specimens:

c.100,000 fossils, 10,000 minerals and rocks; 650 type, figured and referred specimens.

Published catalogues:

Rolfe, W.D.I. et al. 1981. *Type specimens of fossils from the Hunterian Museum and Glasgow Art Gallery and Museum, Glasgow University.* [Microfiche catalogue.] Two articles on the collections by E. Campbell have been published in *The Geological Curator*, **1**, 336-345, 484-485.

Displays:

The main section of the geological displays employs a stratigraphical approach. Each period is represented by a case or series of cases and includes a range of typical fossils. Mineral displays included Scottish material from Strontian, Leadhills and the Clyde Plateau Lavas and a small fluorescent mineral exhibit. Other topics covered include rocks and their classification, the local geology and horse evolution. A complete ichthyosaur skeleton is accompanied by a full-size model. This is one of a series of large scale models of amphibians, reptiles and dinosaurs. The museum's permanent displays are currently under review and may change in the near future.

Staff:

Geology forms part of the Department of Science in which there are 7 curatorial staff. Senior Curator, Dr Darryl Mead, PhD,BSc; Curator with responsibility for Geology, A.H. Gunning, BSc, AMA.

Other information:

The museum has recently assumed responsibility for the management of the Fossil Grove in Victoria Park, Glasgow. This will be carried out on behalf of the Fossil Grove Trust, a charitable body set up to promote and develop this internationally important geological site.

Compiler:

A.H. Gunning

SCOTLAND
GLASGOW
Hunterian Museum

Address:
The University, Glasgow G12 8QQ. Telephone 041 339 8855; Fax 041 307 8059.

Administration:
The Hunterian is a university museum supervised by a Museum Committee. There is a Director responsible for the running of both the Hunterian Museum and Art Gallery. The Professor of Geology is Honorary Keeper of the Geological Collections, and the geology section of the museum has access to the facilities of the teaching department as well as to service departments of the university (e.g. Computing, Photography, Library).

Admission:
Free.

Times of opening:
Monday - Saturday 09.30 - 17.00.

History:

The Hunterian Museum is the oldest museum in Scotland and one of the oldest in the UK. It was opened to the Glasgow public in 1807, but had been available to scholars in London since 1770 at William Hunter's purpose-built museum in Great Windmill Street.

The founder:

William Hunter, FRS (1718-1783), a Glasgow University graduate, became Physician Extraordinary (i.e. obstetrician) to Queen Charlotte and first Professor of Anatomy to the Royal Academy. He was an influential figure in eighteenth century science - e.g. nominating J.A. de Luc, the first to use the word "geology" in English, for his FRS. Hunter was a renowned anatomist, physician, teacher and scholar who built up large collections in many fields of interest, as well as an outstanding library that also survives. His geological collections predominate in minerals (about 3000 specimens), but he also had a fragment of Pallas's meteorite (collected before its extra-terrestrial origin was accepted) as well as Vesuvian basalts, reflecting his interest in the Volcanist debate. Rocks from Captain Cook's voyages are present in the form of artefacts. Hunter was the first to prove extinction in large mammals, with his 1768 paper on the mastodon and in his recently published manuscript on the Irish "elk". This was a significant contribution to Enlightenment thought since it broke the "Great Chain of Being", the pre-evolu-

Earth ... Life *Exhibition, Main Hall*

tionary concept unifying natural science. Hunter also possessed a very fine collection of corals, important as land forming agents in contemporary theories of the Earth. William is often confused with his younger brother John, founder of the Hunterian Museum of the Royal College of Surgeons, London.

Principal collections:

Further details of the following collections will be found in Cleevely, R.J. 1983. World Palaeontological Collections, British Museum (Natural History) and Mansell Publishing, as well as in Stace, H.E., Pettitt, C.W.A. and Waterston, C.D. 1987. Natural Science Collections in Scotland, National Museums of Scotland: Aitken, W.G., Anderson, J.G.C., Bailey, Sir E.B., Begg, J.L., Bell, A., Bowes, D.R., Brown, T. of Waterhaughs and Lanfine, Caldwell, W.G.E., Clark, R.F., Conacher, H.R.J., Crosskey, H.W., Currie, E.D., Dairon, J., Day, J.T., Dix, E., Eagar, R.M.C., Eck, F.A., Ferguson, D., Fox, J., Glenday, Sir V.G., Gregory, J.W., Grierson, T.B., Gwinnell, W.F., Harrison, J.V., Henderson, S.M.K., Hudleston, W.F. Hunter, W., Hutton, A.N., Kidston, R., King, B.C., Lamont, A., Leeds, A.N., Leitch, D., Long, A.G., McCallien, W.J., Macdonald, D., Mackenzie, Sir G.S., McKinnon Wood, M., MacLennan, R.M., Macnair, P., Morton, N., Nicol, W., Padget, P., Pratt, A., Rankin, D.R., Robertson, D., Rutley, F., Seymour, Lord Webb and Playfair, J., Smellie, J.W., Spath, L.F., Thoms, A., Thomson, J., Tripp, R.P., Trueman, Sir A.E., Tutcher, J.W., Tyrrell, G.W., Ure, D., Walton, J., Weir, J., Whymper, E, Whyte, F., Wilson, H.H., Wordie, Sir J.M., Wyllie, B.K.N., Young, J. & J. Following the recent UFC Earth Science Review and merger of university geology departments, the Hunterian now houses the geological collections from Dundee and

Strathclyde universities. A major collection of rocks from Jan Mayen has also been transferred from Birkbeck College, London.

Major strengths:

Mavor, Coulson and Conacher's collection of coals, oil shales and related products; zeolites from the Midland Valley of Scotland; Leadhills – Wanlockhead minerals, Greenockite, minerals from classical European localities; economic rocks and minerals; fresh-water mussels from the Scottish Coal Measures; fossils from Palaeozoic rocks of the Girvan district, Ayrshire; early African and other collections from many parts of the world, the results of expeditions by Professor J.W. Gregory, and described in his books; the Crosskey collection of Quaternary shells, especially of the Firth of Clyde; the Ure Collection of Lanarkshire Carboniferous fossils, described in 1793 in the earliest significant account of Scottish palaeontology; part of the A.N. Leeds collection of fossil reptiles from the Oxford Clay; rocks from the "Discovery" and other expeditions to Antarctica; rocks from Glen Tilt, collected by Lord Seymour at the beginning of the 19th century to illustrate Hutton's proof of the intrusive nature of igneous rocks; minerals from the Hunter, Eck and Rutley collections; some of the first thin sections ever made, by Nicol of Nicol-prism fame; the Kidston collection of fossil plant thin sections, including the famed Rhynie Chert material and Mesozoic royal ferns.

Number of specimens:

c.800,000, including several thousand type specimens.

Published catalogues:

Calder, M. 1960. *Catalogue of the Kidston Collection of sections of fossil plants in the Department of Botany of the University of Glasgow*, University of Glasgow; Currie, E.D. and George, T.N. 1963. Catalogue of described and figured specimens in the Begg collection in the Hunterian Museum of the University of Glasgow, *Palaeontology* **6**, 378-396; Gregory, J.W. and Currie, E.D. 1928. The vertebrate fossils from the Glacial and associated Post-glacial beds of Scotland in the Hunterian Museum, *Monograph of the Geological Department of the Hunterian Museum* **2**; Hopping, C.A. 1957. *Catalogue of fossil plants in the Hunterian Museum of the University of Glasgow*, University of Glasgow; Laskey, J. 1813. *A general account of the Hunterian Museum, Glasgow*, J. Smith & Son, Glasgow; Monographs of the Geological Department of the Hunterian Museum (five volumes published 1925-1938, four on African collections); Rolfe, W.D.I., Ingham, J.K., Currie, E.D., Neville, S., Brannan, J. and Campbell, E. 1981. *Type specimens of fossils from the Hunterian Museum and Glasgow Art Gallery and Museum*, Glasgow University [Microfiche catalogue]; Walton, J. (date unknown). *Index to the collection of sections and preparations of fossil plants: John Walton Collection*, University of Glasgow.

Other publications:

Durant, G.P. and Rolfe, W.D.I. 1984. William Hunter (1718-1783) as a natural historian: his "geological" interests, *Earth Sciences History* **3**, 9-24.

Displays:

The museum is currently undergoing its most extensive renovations in over 100 years. At present, the *Earth ... Life* exhibition provides a framework for a wide range of innovative specimen-based displays. These include meteorites, rocks and minerals, trilobites from the George Rae collection, dinosaur remains (including eggs and tracks), early hominids, and fossils from the Ladyburn Starfish Bed, Lesmahagow, East Kirkton, Bearsden (including the famous Shark), and the Oxford Clay.

Education:

The geological collections are used widely in teaching, not only to undergraduates and for research at other institutions, but also by the museum's education service for primary and secondary school activities. Boxes of material relevant to the Scottish geological syllabus are available for loan to local schools. All the geological curators teach in the university geology department as well as undertaking extra-mural lecturing.

Staff:

Deputy Director, Graham P. Durant, BSc, PhD, FGS; Senior Curator, J. Keith Ingham, BSc, PhD, FGS; Curators, Neil D.L. Clark, BSc, PhD, John W. Faithful, BSc, PhD; Technicians, Michael Jewkes; Gavin Tough.

Compilers:

G.P. Durant & J.W. Faithfull.

SCOTLAND
INVERNESS
Inverness Museum and Art Gallery

Address:
Castle Wynd, Inverness, IV2 3ED. Telephone 0463 237114; Fax 0463 712850.

Administration:
Department of Leisure and Recreation, Inverness District Council.

Admission:
Free. School parties should be booked in advance.

Times of opening:
Monday - Saturday 09.00 - 17.00. Closed on some winter public holidays.

History:
The museum was effectively founded in the collections of the Northern Institution for the Promotion of Science and Literature which were begun in about 1825. Hugh Miller (1802-1856) was a contributor to this society. After a decline in this group in the mid 1830's the collections were transferred to storage at Inverness Royal Academy where they suffered some neglect before being passed to the care of Inverness Burgh Council in about 1865. With the advent of Inverness Scientific Society and Field Club in 1875, interest in the collections was re-awakened and the club took over their pastoral care from the Burgh. Many of the early investigations were directed towards local geology and hence the bulk of the museum's present collection dates from this period, with only a few specimens being identified with the Northern Institution. In the 1880's, under the guidance of John Horne (1848-1928), permanent public displays were developed. In 1906 the Town Council again took over the running of the museum. The old museum was demolished in the early 1960's and the present building erected on the same site. All of the geological material is housed in this building.

Principal collections:
John Horne (1848-1928); Thomas Wallace (1841-1926); James Fraser (d.1929); Baroness Burdett-Coutts (1814-1906); Gordon Sutherland; H.W. Burgess; Angus J. Beaton (active 1880's); William Jolly (d.1912); Inverness Scientific Society and Field Club.

Archives:
Some material relating to Hugh Miller (1802-1856).

Major strengths:
Old Red Sandstone fossil fishes.

Number of specimens:
c. 2,500.

Displays:
Small permanent display dealing with highland minerals, the Great Glen Fault and fossil fish. Temporary exhibitions have included material from the reserve collections plus touring exhibitions from other agencies.

Public services:
The museum's programme includes lunch time lectures and activities which occasionally cover Geological subjects. There is an enquiry service for the identification of specimens.

Research facilities:
Small library and binocular microscope available.

Education:
School loan boxes available.

Staff:
Assistant Curator (Natural Sciences), Stephen Moran, BSc, FRES, AMA.

Compiler:
S. Moran.

SCOTLAND
MONTROSE
Montrose Museum

Address:
Panmure Place, Montrose, DD10 8HE. Telephone 0674 73232; Fax 0307 64834.

Administration:
Montrose Museum is now administered by Angus District Libraries and Museum Service, Angus District Council.

Admission:
Free.

Times of opening:
Monday - Saturday 10.00 - 17.00.

History:

Montrose Museum was established by Montrose Natural History and Antiquarian Society in 1836. It now also contains the geological collections from Arbroath Museum (established 1843), Forfar Museum (established 1898) and Brechin Museum (established 1846).

Principal collections:

The Mitchell Collection of Lower Old Red Sandstone fish and arthropod fossils (returned from the Royal Scottish Museum in 1981); the Howden Collection of glacial and post-glacial fossils; the Lord Gray Agate Collection; the Munich European fossil collection; trace fossils and plant fossils of the Lower Old Red Sandstone.

Major strengths:

Comprehensive collection of fossils including the Munich, Howden and Mitchell Collections; comprehensive mineral collections.

Number of specimens:

Upwards of 8,000 specimens all catalogued and card indexed. Few type and figured specimens.

Displays:

Displays on volcanoes, agates, Lower Old Red Sandstone fossils and glaciation.

Staff:
Curator, Rachel Eames MA, AMA.

Compiler:
Margaret H. King, BSc, AMA.

SCOTLAND
NAIRN
Nairn Literary Institute Museum

Address:
Viewfield House, Viewfield, Nairn, IV12 4EE.

Administration:
Nairn Museum Trust

Admission:
Free.

Times of opening:
June - September: Monday - Saturday 14.30 -16.30.

History:

The Nairn Literary Society was founded by various learned local gentlemen, led by the local practitioner, Dr Grigor. In 1858 a Museum was founded by this Society and housed with the Literary Institute Library in the Public Hall. For many years after the Second World War the collection was housed in Viewfield House, a property originally belonging to Nairn Town Council and since 1975 to Nairn District Council. When additional accommodation became available in the same building in the early 1980's, the collection was transferred and re-displayed and was re-opened to the public in June 1985.

Pricipial collections:

Minerals and rocks donated by Brodie of Brodie (2,000 specimens). This includes important material from Colonel Imrie, the Duchess of Gordon and Sir Charles Giesecke. There is also a very significant collection of local Old Red Sandstone fish fossils (400 specimens) presented in 1887. Also two small collections from Australia.

Number of specimens:

c. 3,000.

Staff:

Honorary Curator, Alan J. McGowan.

Compiler:

A.J. McGowan.

SCOTLAND
PERTH
Perth Museum and Art Gallery

Address:
78 George Street, Perth PH1 5LB. Telephone 0738 32488.

Administration:
Perth and Kinross District Council.

Admission:
Free.

Times of opening:
Monday - Saturday 10.00 - 17.00.

History:

The beginnings of the museum go back to 1784 with the founding of the Literary and Antiquarian Society of Perth. Due to unsuitable housing many of the early natural history specimens perished. In 1823 the Marshall Monument was built, which forms the basis of today's museum building.

In 1867 Dr Francis Buchanan White founded the Perthshire Society of Natural Science (PSNS) which in 1881 built its own museum in Tay Street with much larger and better collections in Natural History than that of the Literary and Antiquarian Society. In 1914, due to a variety of problems, the Literary and Antiquarian Society offered its Natural History specimens to the city and its own museum ceased to exist.

The PSNS eventually appointed a curator, but the expense proved to be excessive and in 1902, after negotiations with the Town Council, the museum and its collections were passed to the city.

In the 1930s new galleries were built next to the Marshall Monument and in 1935 the Perth Museum and Art Gallery was opened by the Duke and Duchess of York.

The museum now contains three curatorial sections: Natural Sciences, Human History and Fine & Applied Arts.

Principal collections

Specimens collected by Peter Macnair, author of *Geology and Science of the Grampians*, and a curator of the Natural History Collections in Glasgow Museums; some fish specimens from Hugh Mitchell (1882-1894) including type specimens; small collection of Silurian fossils from Gotland, from Robert Dunlop (1848-1921), a curator of Pittencrieff Park Museum, Dunfermline; T.M. Barr (d.1903) fossil collection, engineer to Caledonian Railway; Henry Coates Collection, a curator of Perth Museum; C.F. Davidson Collection, cited and figured material from the Arctic Clay of Errol, Perthshire.

Major strengths:

Relatively good collection of local Lower Old Red Sandstone fossil fish and plants; Arctic Clay fossils from Errol, Perthshire.

Number of specimens:

c.2,500 minerals, c.1,600 fossils, c.1,500 rocks; c.30 type, figured and cited specimens.

Displays:

1984 Natural History Gallery on the geology, flora and fauna of Perthshire.

Staff:

Keeper of Natural Sciences, Mike Taylor, BSc, AMA; Assistant Keeper of Natural Sciences, Anne Abernethy, BSc, AMA.

Compiler:

Anne Abernethy.

WALES
CARDIFF
National Museum of Wales

Address:
Cathays Park, Cardiff, South Glamorgan CF1 3NP. Telephone 0222 397951.

Administration:
National Museum funded by grants-in-aid from the Treasury via the Welsh Office, administered through a Court of Governors and Council.

Admission:
Adults £2.50; children (5–15 years) £1.25; under 5 years free; senior citizens, unemployed, disabled £1.85; groups, including school parties, by special arrangement; single, double and family season tickets available; special charges for temporary exhibitions.

Times of opening:
Tuesday - Saturday 10.00 - 17.00, Sunday 14.30 - 17.00, closed Monday (except Bank Holidays), Christmas Eve, Christmas Day, Boxing Day, New Year's Day, Good Friday, May Day.

History:
Royal Charter granted in March 1907. The foundation stone for the first phase of the main building was laid in June 1912 by King George V, who also performed the formal opening ceremony in April 1927. From 1912 until 1921 the National Museum occupied a building on the site of the adjacent City Hall, where temporary exhibitions were displayed, and then from 1922 onwards part of the new building was occupied and opened informally to the public prior to its formal completion. The original collections incorporated those of the Cardiff Municipal Museum (established 1868), which were transferred to the new National Musuem at the first meeting of the Court of Governors in 1912.

Principal collections:
For curatorial and research purposes the primary collections are maintained within two sections in the Department of Geology - a Palaeontology Section and a Mineralogy/Petrology Section. The reserve and study fossil collections are extensive and international in scope, but with some emphasis on Palaeozoic material from Wales and the Welsh Borderland and on Jurassic faunas from South Wales and Dorset. Major strengths are in Lower Palaeozoic brachiopods and trilobites; Upper Silurian-

Diorama and dinosaurs in the Evolution of Wales *exhbition*

Devonian plants, including crucial early vascular floras; Lower Carboniferous shelly faunas; Upper Carboniferous (Coal Measures) bivalves and plants, including comprehensive ecological collections; and Lower Jurassic (Liassic) invertebrates, especially ammonites. Comparative international collections are especially strong in brachiopods and trilobites, particularly from the Baltic area. The Department also houses for safe keeping 30 ichthyosaur skeletons from the Lower Jurassic of Somerset and Dorset, which form part of the Charles Moore Collection belonging to the Bath Royal Literary and Scientific Institute. Type, figured and referred fossils are numerous.

The mineral collections comprise a definitive database for Welsh mineralogy, including a wide range of specimens of gold, brookite, anatase, millerite and anglesite, etc. Other extensive material is from world-wide localities. Incorporated into the main collections is the R.J. King Collection which, when acquired in 1985, represented one of the most substantial and finest suites of minerals in private hands in the UK; this collection is especially rich in coverage of material from the north of England and

Cornwall. Suites of rocks are mostly from Welsh localities.

Archives:

A third curatorial section (Documentation) within the department is responsible for archives and associated documentation. Geological and topographical map coverage is complete at all scales for Wales, with wide representation also for other areas of the British Isles. There is a significant collection of antiquarian maps. Among the historical archive, the correspondence, papers, notes and drawings of Henry Thomas de la Beche form one of the main sources of data relating to the early nineteenth-century development of geology in the British Isles, and especially to the origins of the Geological Survey. Other archival collections relate to such well-known geologists as F.J. North, B.B. Bancroft, A.H. Cox and T.N. George.

Published catalogues:

North, F.J. 1928. Type and figured fossils in the National Museum of Wales. *Geological Magazine*, **65**, 193-210 [reprinted in the same year as a Museum publication with pagination 1-20].

Bassett, M.G. 1972. *Catalogue of type, figured and cited fossils in the National Museum of Wales*. National Museum of Wales, Cardiff.

Bevins, R.E. and Horak, J.M. 1994. *Catalogue of the R.J. King Mineral Collection in the National Museum of Wales*. National Museum of Wales Geological Series No. 11, Cardiff.

Owens, R.M. and Bassett, M.G. 1994. *Catalogue of type, figured and cited fossils in the National Museum of Wales: Supplement 1972-1993*. National Museum of Wales Geological Series No. 12, Cardiff.

Other publications:

Academic monographs, catalogues, field-excursion guides and booklets on "popular" aspects of geology are published irregularly as the Geological Series of the National Museum of Wales. A catalogue of currently available titles is available on request from the Bookshop Manager.

Displays:

Major new Earth Science galleries were opened in October 1993. These occupy over 1,200 square metres dedicated mostly to a single exhibition entitled *The Evolution of Wales*. Apart from incorporating numerous specimens from the Museum collections, this display involves the extensive use of film, videos and sound to illustrate integrated geological and biological processes from the origins of the Earth to the present day. The exhibition is essentially a "walk through time" divided into 8 modules or "pods" that illustrate various segments of Earth history with some emphasis on the record preserved in Wales. Smaller adjacent galleries illustrate processes and diversity of rocks, fossils, minerals and modern animals and plants. There is an active programme of temporary exhibitions which has recently included a number of major dinosaur displays and also *Mammoths and the Ice Age* and *Prehistoric Sea Monsters*.

Public services:

The Department of Geology maintains a full enquiry service at all levels of academic and "public" scope. Access to the library and map collections is available as part of this service, as is consultation of the reserve geological collections by bona fide research workers. Loans for scientific study are made world-wide on request. Schools enquiries are normally channelled through the Museum Schools Service, where there is a geologically qualified officer in charge of educational programmes. During the summer there is a series of guided walks through various areas of Wales as part of a wider Museum programme entitled "Discovering Wales".

Research facilities:

The Department houses a complete range of equipment for research in palaeontology, mineralogy and petrology, including X-ray and SEM facilities. New preparation and conservation laboratories were opened in 1991. There is also a comprehensive geological library in addition to the Museum's central library, which houses a further range of relevant general publications.

Current projects:

Computerization of register data is a long-term curatorial programme within a specially funded overall Museum Documentation Project. Research in palaeontology is currently on trilobite and brachiopod studies, including revisions of British Ordovician faunas, Carboniferous trilobites and Ordovician-Silurian brachiopods from the Anglo-Baltic area, the description of new Tournaisian silicified brachiopods from South

Wales, and revisionary work for the brachiopod and trilobite volumes of the *Treatise on invertebrate palaeontology*. There is also an ongoing study of the interpretation of late Triassic reptilian footprints. Mineralogical and petrological research includes the compilation of a mineral data bank for Wales, and studies of low-grade metamorphism, volcanic processes, the origin of gneissose terranes etc.

Staff:

Keeper, M.G. Bassett, BSc, PhD, DSc, FMA, CGeol, FGS; Assistant Keeper (Palaeontology), R.M. Owens, BSc, PhD, FRAS, CGeol, FGS; Assistant Keeper (Mineralogy/Petrology), R.E. Bevins, BSc, PhD, CGeol, FGS. There is a current total curatorial and support staff complement of 17, of whom 13 have degree qualifications in geology. Five Honorary Research Associates also contribute materially to the work of the Department.

Other information:

The Department of Geology, University of Wales College of Cardiff, is in the building adjacent to the Museum, within a few minutes walk; full research and library facilities are available at the university, where there are currently over 30 teaching and research staff in geology. A number of Museum staff are Honorary Lecturers in the university.

Compiler:

M.G. Bassett.

NORTHERN IRELAND
BELFAST
Ulster Museum

Address:
Botanic Gardens, Belfast, BT9 5AB. Telephone 0232 381251; Fax 0232 665510.

Admission:
Free.

Times of opening:
Monday - Friday 10.00 - 17.00, Saturday 13.00 - 17.00, Sunday 14.00 - 17.00.

History:

Founded in 1831 as the Belfast Museum by the Belfast Natural History and Philosophical Society. A second geological collection was established in the Belfast Museum and Art Gallery in 1890 by the Belfast Town Council and the two collections merged when the Society agreed to transfer its collection to the city by deed of gift in 1910. In 1929 the collections were transferred to the new Belfast Museum and Art Gallery run by the Belfast Corporation. In 1962 the Northern Ireland Government took control of the building and collections handed over by Belfast City as set out in the terms of the Museum Act (Northern Ireland) of the preceding year. The geological collections were curated within the Department of Natural History up to 1970 when a new Department of Geology was established by implementation of recommendations following a government inspection.

Principal collections:

G.A.N. Arber - fossil plants; W.H. Baily -Irish fossils (Geological Survey of Ireland); A.H.I. Baker - mostly British fossils, minerals and rocks; R.W. Barstow - world-wide minerals; Belfast Natural History and Philosophical Society - wide ranging geological collections with a predominantly Irish interest; Belfast Naturalists' Field Club - predominantly Ulster geological collections; A. Bell - Irish Quaternary molluscs; R. Bell - Ulster geological material, particularly minerals; R.B. Bennett - Carboniferous reef faunas chiefly from County Kildare; M.C. Boulter - Tertiary spores from Lough Neagh Basin; S.A. Brenan - world-wide minerals; J. Brennan - Irish minerals; British Association for the Advancement of Science - Irish geological photograph albums; H. Brunton

Edmontosaurus annectens *from the Cretaceous of South Dakota*

- silicified Carboniferous faunas from County Fermanagh; W. Buckland - correspondence; C. Bulla - Northern Ireland Carboniferous fossil fish; W. Bullock - Northern Ireland graptolites; R. Byrne - County Antrim Jurassic vertebrates; Caledon Collection - world-wide minerals; J.W. Carr; W.D. Christianson - world-wide minerals; A. McI.Cleland - Ulster rocks, particularly flints; W.W. Cole - see Enniskillen; H. Corke - world-wide minerals; W.S. Darley - British and Irish minerals; M. Davis - world-wide minerals, particularly garnets and gemstones; A. Davison - British and Irish minerals; C. Davison - Irish Mesozoic fossils; P. Doran - early collections, chiefly Irish; P.S. Doughty - wide ranging, but especially British and Irish Carboniferous fossils; D. Dunlop - French minerals; P. de M.G. Egerton - correspondence; Third Earl of Enniskillen - correspondence; J. Finnegan - Irish fossils and minerals; H.J. Foy - Irish minerals; T. Galloway; D.H. Garske - world-wide minerals; W. Gault - Northern Ireland Cretaceous fossils; Gemmological Supplies - gemstones; Geological Survey of Ireland (pre-1922) - material from the six counties of Northern Ireland; Geological Survey of Northen Ireland - some Northern Ireland specimens and equipment; Geomar - North American and Australian minerals; S.R.R. Gilmore - Irish fossils; D.S. Graham -world-wide minerals; T.B. Graham - Irish fossils; J. Grainger - a founding collection of British and Irish material; W. Gray - Irish fossils; M.C.A. Green - Irish fossils; W.A. Green - Irish Mesozoic fossils; R.J. Griffith - Irish geological maps; J. Hanna - minerals; Irish Base Metals - suites of Irish minerals; J.W. Jackson - correspondence, notebooks, Irish geological photographs, County Antrim Quaternary vertebrates; A. Jeram - fossil arthropods; T. Johnston; J.B. Jukes - correspondence and map; A. Kennedy; C. Kerr - Silurian status trace fossil assemblages from County Down; L.G. de Koninck - European Carboniferous fossils; C. Lapworth - correspondence and manuscripts; B.S. Lloyd - world-wide minerals and fossils; J. MacAdam - Irish fossils; C.C. Marshall - Northern Ireland Mesozoic fossils; T. Mason - Carboniferous fossils from County Fermanagh; R McDonald - Northern Ireland Mesozoic fossils; F. M'Coy - correspondence; T. McE. Megaw - largely British and Irish minerals; W.F. Millett - Holocene gastropods; The Mineral Gallery - world-wide minerals and fossils; C. Morrice - North American echinoids; G.H. Morton; M.F. Mulholland - English minerals; R. Murdoch - world-wide minerals; R. Nash - English fossils; R. Nawaz - Irish minerals and rocks, Pakistani minerals and gemstones; D. Nevin - Australian minerals; F. Olaloye - Irish Carboniferous bryozoans including status material; R. Old - Northern Ireland minerals, chiefly zeolites; Mrs Ormsby - minerals; R.J. Orr - Irish fossil ostracods including status material; Pakenham Collection - world-wide minerals; J. Parkin - Irish, chiefly County Kerry, Silurian fossils; People's Palace Museum, Belfast -Irish material; A. G. Pomeroy - British and Irish minerals; J.E. Portlock - Irish fossils and rocks including much status material; J. Preston - rocks and minerals; Queen's University of Belfast - geological specimens, largely fossils; W. Reed - Irish Carboniferous fossils; C.G.R. Reid - English and Irish fossils and minerals; R.E.H. Reid - fossil sponges, chiefly Cretaceous, from Britain and Ireland including much status material, plus Mesozoic fossil vertebrates; H. Robinson - Irish Tertiary and Quaternary molluscs; Rough Gems - minerals and gemstones; Royal Dublin Society; Royal School Armagh - Irish fossils; A. Sedgwick - correspondence; J. Shanks - Northern Ireland graptolites; W. Smith - map; I.D. Somerville - Carboniferous faunas from North Wales; Sotheby's - minerals and fossils; G. Spinelli - Italian minerals and Tertiary fossils; S.A. Stewart - Irish Quaternary molluscs and fossil plants; Stone Science - world-wide minerals; W. Swanston - Ordovician and Silurian graptolites from Northen Ireland, manuscripts and personalia; Tara Mines - suites of Irish minerals; R. Tate - Northern Ireland Mesozoic fossils; R. Tavener-Smith - Carboniferous and Recent bryozoans including status material; Richard Taylor Minerals - world-wide minerals; S.J. Thompson - Australian minerals; G.D. de la Touche - world-wide minerals, some fossils; M.J. Townsend - Peruvian minerals; R.W. Tscernich - North American zeolites; Ulster Museum Geological Recording Group - Carboniferous fossils and minerals from Northern Ireland; Mrs Viapree - Brazilian gemstones; Ward's Natural Science Establishment Inc. - world-wide minerals and fossils; R.J. Welch - geological photographs, Quaternary molluscs, manuscripts and personalia; S. Weller - world-wide minerals; J. Whittaker - Irish Mesozoic marine vertebrates; J. Wilson - Carboniferous fossils, largely from Northern Ireland, predominantly foraminiferans; World Wide Mineralogical Company - fluorescent minerals; J. Wright - microfossils, particularly foraminiferans, plus Irish Carboniferous and Mesozoic fossils; S. Wright - world-wide minerals; R. Young - Irish geological material.

Archives:

There is a library of early and rare geological books, with emphasis on Irish geology, local economic geology and biography (around 400 volumes and growing). The collection of geological offprints, currently around 3,000 in number, is available to visitors as is the transparency collection of around 8,400 frames. There is also a small collection of prints and drawings including the work of Neave Parker.

Major strengths:

Irish Jurassic and Cretaceous faunas. Carboniferous Limestone faunas, particularly corals, brachiopods and foraminiferans (mainly Irish). Irish Quaternary faunas (vertebrates and molluscs). Fossil sponges, particularly from the Upper Cretaceous. Repository of historical and heritage collections such as the early Geological Survey of Ireland material. Mineralogy strengths include garnets (>1,000 specimens), silica minerals (1,500 specimens), zeolites (800 specimens), and carbonates (400 specimens). There is an outstanding gemstone collection of around 1,000 items.

Number of specimens:

c.200,000 fossils probably represented by 30,000 records when computerised documentation is complete (including about 900 status specimens); c. 25,000 minerals represented by 14,000 records (including two holotypes in the sense of Embrey and Hey (1968); c. 3,000 rocks in addition to over 700 metres of drill cores.

Published catalogues:

Tunnicliff, S.P. 1980. *A catalogue of the Lower Palaeozoic fossils in the collection of Major-General J.E. Portlock, etc.* Ulster Museum, Belfast.

James, K.W. *et al.* 1983. *A list of the photographs in the R.J. Welch Collection in the Ulster Museum. Volume 2. Botany, Geology and Zoology.* Ulster Museum, Belfast.

Other publications:

Ulster Museum Souvenir Guide. Ulster Museum, Belfast. A complete catalogue of the mineral collection and partial catalogues of the palaeontology collections are available in computer printout form by arrangement.

Displays:

The Earth in Space: a small presentation introducing time, space, the universe, our galaxy and solar system, the early evolution of the earth and the origins of life.

The Variety of Life: an integrated palaeontological and biological display treating the diversity of the animal and plant kingdoms in their major taxonomic groupings using large numbers of specimens, some of very large size, with many wax models in unconventional presentation.

The Historical Geology of Ireland: an exploration of the evolution of the geology of Ireland, period by period, showing the principal rocks and fossils of the island. Major features of the gallery are a press-button, illuminating geological map of Ireland, dioramas with sound commentaries, a 'technamated' section through a volcano, pictorial restorations of early Irish landscapes and a mounted skeleton of a Giant Irish Deer.

The Restless Land: a presentation of some important topographical features and the processes which formed them. Features are a cast of part of a sea-cliff and full-size replica of a limestone cave with formations.

Earth's Treasures: a mineral gallery in which large numbers of fine specimens are shown in a dark environment. Of particular note are a giant quartz group from Arkansas, some fine gemstones, and a presentation of fluorescent, phosphorescent and radioactive minerals in a small central 'theatre'.

The Dinosaur Show: a family exhibition in the central atrium of the museum built around the original skeleton of *Edmontosaurus annectens*, explaining some of the simple concepts essential for the understanding of dinosaurs. Two cartoon characters conduct the visitor around the gallery and all main labels are in the form of bubble captions conforming to a comprehension and reading age of between 8 and 9.

Many of these exhibitions are likely to be affected by major gallery reorganisation over the next few years.

There is also a temporary and travelling exhibitions programme generating exhibitions on a regular basis. Enquiries should be made to the Keeper.

Staff:

Head of Sciences Division, P.S. Doughty, MSc, FMA, FGS; Keeper of Geology, post vacant; Curator (Palaeontology), A. Jeram, MA, PhD; Curator (Mineralogy/Petrology), R. Nawaz, MSc, PhD, FGA; Senior Museum Assistant, K.W. James, BSc; Personal Secretary, Miss M. Keenan.

Other information:

The Department is the only museum geology provision in Northern Ireland. Other geological resources in close proximity are the Geological Survey of Northern Ireland, 20 College Gardens, Belfast (300 metres) and Queen's University Geology Department (400 metres).

Compiler:

P.S. Doughty.

REPUBLIC OF IRELAND
CORK
Cork Geological Museum

Address:
Geology Department, University College, Cork. Telephone 010 353 21 276871; Fax 010 353 21 275948.

Administration:
A University Museum, funded by the Geology Department. Current work is being sponsored by FAS, the Government Training Agency. The Museum is administered by the Cork Geological Museum Committee which consists of members of the academic, curatorial and local communities.

Admission:
Free.

Times of opening:
The Museum is open daily for research workers and for departmental teaching. There are several open days for the public throughout the year. At all other times viewing is by appointment only.

History:
The original collections date back to the foundation of the College in 1849, when the Geological Survey of Ireland presented a representative set of Irish rocks, minerals and fossils. At around the same time purchases from Krantz of Bonn began, and these included many European mineral and fossil specimens. Various private donations were made during the late 19th century. The original Museum, shared with Natural History, Botany and Zoology, was located in the North Wing. In the 1920's demand for space in the College led to the gradual reduction and eventual closure of the Museum. The collections were put into storage or given away. On completion of the new Science Building in 1967 a small amount of material was again put on display. The Museum in its present state was established in 1981.

Principal collections:
Charles Coote Grant Collection of Silurian fossils from Ontario; Lady Windle Collection; General O'Leary Collection; O'Donohue Collection of minerals; K.T. Higgs Collection of Carboniferous and Devonian miospores, John S. Jackson Collection.

Archaeopteris hibernica *from the Upper Devonian Kiltorcan Formation*

Archives:
The archives include a full set of Irish 1" geological maps, the majority with memoirs; over 2,000 other maps, including a set of 5 hand-coloured, signed and dated Townland Index maps (including the first publications of the Geological Survey of Ireland, dating from 1848); an extensive offprint collection with emphasis on Irish geology; the John S. Jackson Collection (over 4,000 items), including many rare items mainly related to Ireland, and now housed in the John S. Jackson Library; aerial photographs (Geological Survey of Ireland 1967 and Air Corps); photographic slides with emphasis on Irish geology, but including photomicrographs of moon rock.

Major strengths:
The collections are housed in 3 locations within the Department of Geology and are divided into minerals, fossils, rocks and archives. The collections are extensive and international in scope, but with an emphasis on material from Ireland. There is an important collection of plant material from the Upper Devonian Kiltorcan Formation, including superb specimens of *Archaeopteris hibernica*. The Museum is currently building up a large microfossil collection, which is particularly strong in Devonian and Carboniferous miospores. Type, figured and referred material is included in the collections, for example the type specimen of the gem quality quartz variety, Cotterite from Rockforest, Mallow, Co. Cork.

Publications:

Museum guides and field excursion guides are published occasionally.

Displays:

There are 24 display cases on permanent exhibition. Temporary public exhibitions are shown at least once a year, for example on Irish Geology Day.

Public services:

The Department of Geology maintains a full enquiry service at all levels of academic and public requirements. Access to the collections is available as part of this service. Loans for specific study are made. School enquiries and visits are catered for, and a museum loan set is available to schools. A series of field trips is offered during the year, particularly associated with Irish Geology Day. Exhibitions are mounted occasionally for a wider public audience.

Research facilities:

The Museum is housed in the Geology Department which has a wide range of equipment for research in mineralogy, petrology and micropalaeontology.

Current projects:

The Museum is currently undergoing an intensive cataloguing and curating programme sponsored by the Government Training Agency, FAS. The data is being stored, using Apple Macintosh computers with Filemaker Pro software. Catalogues can be produced in various formats, and tailored to meet specific requirements. The data records are compatible with those of the National Museum of Ireland and The Geological Survey of Ireland and it is intended that they will form part of a national geological heritage database. Computer generated catalogues are currently available for much of the archives, for the minerals and fossils, and for a portion of the rock collections.

Other projects include a publicity drive to encourage school use of the Museum and the production of a short video to demonstrate some of its work.

Staff:

No permanent staff. Six temporary staff sponsored by FAS, the Government Training Agency.

Other information:

Other geological resources in close proximity include the Cork City Museum in Fitzgeralds Park.

Compiler:

Bettie Higgs.

REPUBLIC OF IRELAND
DUBLIN
National Museum of Ireland

Address:
Geological Section, 7-9 Merrion Row, Dublin 2. Telephone 010 353 16618811; Fax 010 353 16766116.

Administration:
Department of the Taoiseach, Government Buildings, Upper Merrion Street, Dublin 2.

Admission:
Free.

Times of opening:
Tuesday - Saturday 10.00 - 17.00, Sunday 14.00 - 17.00. By appointment only.

Foundation and history:
State museum founded in 1877 based on older collections of the Royal Dublin Society, Museum of Irish Industry and Royal Irish Academy. The earliest collection is that of Nathanael Leske which dates from 1792 and consists of German minerals. Geological collections were displayed in the Natural History Museum and various annexe buildings until 1922 when the new state parliament was set up in neighbouring Leinster House. Since then the geological collections have been out of sight, moving into storage in suburban Dublin in 1962 and then transferred fifty miles further from the city in 1979. Three posts were created in 1981, two geologists and one technician. All collections are now being concentrated in new stores at Beggars Bush in Dublin beside the Geological Survey of Ireland.

Principal collections:
British Liassic marine reptiles; Irish invertebrate type material; Irish Pleistocene cave and bog bones, particularly Giant Irish Deer; minerals from central Europe, Ireland, Greenland and Iceland; Tertiary plants and invertebrates from Greenland and the Canadian Arctic archipelago; Tertiary mammals from the Siwalik Hills of India.

Number of specimens:
The collections are international with only about 20% of the 100,000 specimens being Irish in origin.

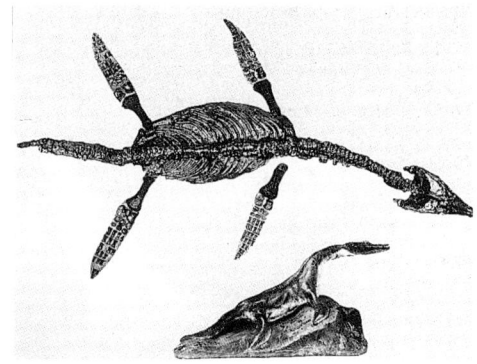

Rhomaleosaurus cramptoni *from the Lias of Whitby*

Published catalogues:
There are several 19th century published catalogues of vertebrates as well as more recent catalogues of meteorites and manuscript catalogues of type material and marine reptiles.

Other publications:
Monaghan, N.T. 1984. The geological collections of the National Museum of Ireland. *Geological Curator*, **3**, 528-536.

Monaghan, N.T. 1992. Geology in the National Museum of Ireland. *Geological Curator*, **5**, 275-282.

Displays:
Exhibition space demolished in 1962 was not replaced. A small exhibition in the Merrion Row building is open when staffing levels permit.

Current projects:
Arrangement of stored collections in new premises at Beggars Bush building, collections data input into computer database, development of displays in Merrion Row.

Staff:
Assistant Keeper (Palaeontology), N.T. Monaghan, BA.

Compiler:
N.T. Monaghan.

REPUBLIC OF IRELAND
DUBLIN
Trinity College Geological Museum

Address:
Department of Geology, Trinity College, Dublin 2.
Telephone 010 353 1 7021477; Fax 010 353 1 6711199.

Administration:
University of Dublin.

Admission:
Free.

Times of opening:
Monday - Friday 10.00 - 16.30. Groups by arrangement with the Curator.

The interior of the Museum Building, showing examples of Irish marbles

History:

The Dublin University Museum (out of which grew the present Geological Museum) was founded in 1777 by the Board of the College to house a series of Polynesian artefacts collected on James Cook's voyages. Its first Curator was the Rev. William Hamilton (1755-1797), a Fellow of the College, who is perhaps best remembered for his *Letters concerning the northern coast of the county of Antrim* (1786). By 1846 the Museum contained geological, zoological and anthropological sections, as well as a herbarium. In 1848 the large geological collections of the Geological Society of Dublin (1831-1890) were donated to the College and further additions caused storage and display problems. From 1857 the geological collections were housed in the purpose built Museum Building (which was designed by Woodward and Deane who were responsible later for the Oxford Museum) where the Geological Museum occupied a large first floor room. In 1956 the need to expand teaching facilities in the Department of Geology resulted in the division of the museum into various laboratories. The Geological Museum now occupies a room at the top of the Museum Building.

Principal collections:

Ainsworth, Nigel - Mesozoic ostracods from offshore Ireland, the Celtic Sea and Fastnet Basins, including much status material; Charlesworth, Edward (1813-1893) - British Natural History Society material; Clayton, Geoffrey - Palaeozoic palynomorphs from Ireland, including some status material; Cole, William Willoughby, Earl of Enniskillen (1807-1886) - Palaeozoic invertebrates from Ireland and England; Foord, Arthur Humphries (1845-1933) - Carboniferous cephalopods from Ireland, including some status material; Graydon, Rev. George - Eocene fish from Monte Bolca, Italy, plus Vesuvius volcanic material (many may be lost); Griffith, Sir Richard (1784-1878) [engineer, geological cartographer, public servant] - reference collection of Carboniferous fossils described by M'Coy (1844), including some syntypes (much missing), plus general collection of Irish minerals (may be lost); Haughton, Major General John (1836-1889) - St. Helena material; Haughton, Rev. Samuel (1821-1897) - Kiltorcan plant material, including status material; Holland, Charles Hepworth - palaeontological symbionts and Silurian invertebrates from Ireland (Dingle Peninsula, County Kerry), England (Ludlow) and China, including some status material; Huxley, Thomas Henry (1825-1895) - material from Jarrow colliery; Joly, John (1857-1933) - general collection of minerals and radioactive minerals from Ireland, Europe and world-wide; Knox, Honourable George [Member of Parliament for Dublin University 1797-1807, before and after the Act of Union of 1800] - general collection of world-wide minerals; Mallet, Robert (1810-1881) [seismologist and engineer] - Italian volcanics (many may be lost); Portlock, Joseph Ellison (1794-1864) - Ordovician and Mesozoic invertebrates from Ireland (counties Derry and Tyrone); Siveter, Derek J. - Silurian trilobites from Ireland (Annascaul inlier, County Kerry), including status material; Smyth, Louis Bouvier (1883-1954) - Carboniferous invertebrates (especially corals and cephalopods) from Ireland (counties Antrim, Donegal, Dublin and Wexford), north Wales (Great Orme's Head), including status material; Wright, Joseph (1834-1923) - Carboniferous crinoids from Ireland, including status material.

Archives:

Handwritten catalogues of early collections including Graydon, Griffith, Knox, Mallet, Perceval Collections; Geological Society of Dublin/Royal Geological Society of Ireland minute books and other manuscript items; George Graydon archives including diary of travels in northern Italy (c.1792); Sir Richard Griffith (1784-1878) archives including four copies of his 6 inch to 1 mile Geological Map to accompany the report of the Railway Commissioners and manuscript catalogue of Carboniferous fossils presented to the Dublin University Museum; John Joly (1857-1933) archives including diaries, manuscripts, research notebooks, some equipment, cameras, black & white lantern slides, colour lantern slides, Devonian fish paintings and stuffed parrot; Leskean Collection archives including manuscript entitled *Synopsis of the arrangement of the Vulcanic Cabinet annexed to the Leskena Collection in the Museum of the Dublin Society*, written on paper watermark dated 1804. This collection was acquired by the Dublin Society in 1792 and is now in the National Museum of Ireland.

Major strengths:

Geological Society of Dublin - c.100 specimens; Kiltorcan plant material - c. 50 specimens, including status material; Ballypalady plant material - Tertiary flora from County Antrim; Carboniferous invertebrates from Ireland - Ball, R., Brennand, T.P., Burns, V., Cox, B.A., Harrison, J., Hudson, R.G.S., Jackson, J.S., Nevill, W.E., Oldham, T., Philcox, M.E., Whitehead, D.; Bryozoans - Buttler, C.J. (from the Ordovician of Ireland and Iran), Bancroft, A.J., Dresser, A.M., Wyse Jackson, P.N. (from the Carboniferous of Ireland and Britain); Cnidaria - Nudds, J.R., Smyth, L.B., Vaughan, A. (from the Carboniferous of Ireland, including status material); Crinoidea - Donovan, S.K., Sevastopulo, G.D. (from the Palaeozoic of Ireland); Foraminifera - Marchant, T.R. (from the Carboniferous of Ireland), Gunn, W.F. (from the Recent of Jamaica, Atlantic and Ireland); Radiolarians - Challenger Expedition 1875;

Ostracoda - Ten Have, M.R. (from the Carboniferous of Ireland); Graptolites - Archer, J.B., Burns, V., Palmer, D.C., Rickards, B.R. (from Ireland); Conodonts - Jackson, P., Johnston, I.S., Jones, G. Ll., Lewis, D., Sevastopulo, G.D., Rees, J., Thornbury, B.M. (from the Carboniferous of Ireland); Fish - from the Jurassic of Solnhofen, Germany and the Oligocene of Glarus, Switzerland; Other vertebrates - *Megaloceros giganteus* (two skeletons, some skulls and assorted bones), *Cervus elaphus* var. *fossilis hibernicus* (skeleton), fragments of dinosaur eggshell, Andrews' Expedition Gobi Desert (Boydell Collection), dinosaur material from Mozambique, some Siwalik material from Doab Canal; Meteorites - 49 specimens, including main mass of Dundrum fall (1865), Adare (Brasky) fragment (1813), and slice of Bovedy (1969) meteorite.

Number of specimens:

70,000 fossils, 15,000 rocks, 7,000 minerals. c. 2,000 status specimens (383 type, 1069 figured, 327 referred to the end of 1988; c. 600 added since).

Published catalogues:

Apjohn, J. 1850. *A descriptive catalogue of the minerals in the Museum of Trinity College Dublin*. M.H. Gill, Dublin.

Ball, V. 1882. Catalogue of the examples of meteoric falls in the museums of Dublin. *Scientific Proceedings of the Royal Dublin Society*, **3** (n.s.), 298-301.

M'Coy, F. 1841. *A catalogue of the Museum of the Geological Society of Dublin*. Hodges and Smith, Dublin, 27pp.

Nudds, J.R. 1982a. Catalogue of type and figured corals from the Geological Museum, Trinity College, Dublin. *Fossil Cnidaria*, **11**, 19-26.

Nudds, J.R. 1982b. Catalogue of type, figured and referred fossils in the Geological Museum of Trinity College Dublin: Part 1. *Journal of Earth Sciences Royal Dublin Society*, **4**, 133-165.

Nudds, J.R. 1982c. Catalogue of type, figured and referred fossils in the Geological Museum of Trinity College Dublin: Part 2. *Ibid.*, **5**, 61-89.

Nudds, J.R. 1983. Catalogue of type, figured and referred fossils in the Geological Museum of Trinity College Dublin: Part 3. *Ibid.*, **5**, 153-190.

Nudds, J.R. 1984. Catalogue of type, figured and referred fossils in the Geological Museum of Trinity College Dublin: Part 4. *Irish Journal of Earth Sciences*, **6**, 47-93.

Nudds, J.R. 1988. Catalogue of type, figured and referred fossils in the Geological Museum of Trinity College Dublin: Supplement (Animalia). *Ibid.*, **9**, 177-196.

Nudds, J.R. 1989. Catalogue of type, figured and referred fossils in the Geological Museum of Trinity College Dublin: Supplement (Plantae). *Ibid.*, **10**, 43-53.

Seymour, H.J. 1951. Catalogue of examples of meteorites in Irish museums. *Scientific Proceedings of the Royal Irish Academy*, **25** (n.s.), 193-199.

Stokes, W. 1807. *A catalogue of the minerals in the Museum of Trinity College*. W. Watson, Dublin.

Stokes, W. 1818. *A descriptive catalogue of the minerals in the systematic collection of the Museum of Trinity College Dublin*. Dublin.

Wyse Jackson, P.N. and Sleeman, A.G. 1990. Return of type, figured, referred and other fossils from the geological collections of Trinity College Dublin to the Geological Survey of Ireland. *Geological Survey of Ireland Bulletin*, **4** (3), 221-222.

Other publications:

Wyse Jackson, P.N. 1992. The Geological Collections of Trinity College, Dublin 1777-1990. *The Geological Curator*, **5**, 263-274.

Displays:

The Museum contains two display areas: the main gallery and the entrance hall of the Museum Building. At present an exhibition, *The Story of the Earth*, is open in the main gallery, and was the Museum's contribution to the celebrations of the 400th birthday of Trinity College. The exhibition serves as an introduction to Geology and consists of over 20 individual displays. These include dinosaur material from Africa, North America and eggshell from Mongolia, meteorites (including three Irish falls), fluorescent minerals, zeolites from the Tertiary of Ireland, gemstones, ichthyosaurs and plesiosaurs from southern Britain, Carboniferous "reef" communities, fossil fish from the Eocene of Italy, Irish industrial products including synthetic diamonds, geological collecting and the history and development of the Geological Museum.

The Entrance Hall of the Museum Building is dominated by two skeletons of *Megaloceras giganteus* the Giant Irish Deer. As well as these skeletons some very good visual material is on display: minerals from the John Joly Collection, and fine fossil specimens including a slab of *Cheirotherium barthii* footprints and a large *Titanites* ammonite. In addition two displays focus on the building itself, and illustrate its architecture and its decorative marbles.

Research facilities:

The museum is located within the Department of Geology, Trinity College, where a wide range of facilities including a comprehensive library is available.

Staff:

Curator, Patrick N. Wyse Jackson, MA, PhD, HdipEd.

Other information:

The Geological Survey of Ireland and the National Museum of Ireland (Geological Section) are both located within 5 minutes of the Museum.

Compiler:

Patrick N. Wyse Jackson.

REPUBLIC OF IRELAND
GALWAY
James Mitchell Museum

Address:
Department of Geology, University College Galway, University Road, Galway. Telephone 010 353 91 24411, ext. 2351; Fax 010 353 91 25700.

Administration:
Funded by small contributions from recurrent class grant to the Department of Geology and small, periodic donations from local business and industry. Curatorial staff are lecturers in the Geology Department and their work in the museum is voluntary.

Admission:
Free.

Times of opening:
Monday - Friday 10.00 - 17.00 during term. Group visits outside term can be made by prior appointment.

History:

Although the College was opened to students in 1849, the museum was initially founded by the Museum Committee to the Council of Queen's College Galway, probably during 1851, through donations from funds allocated to the chairs of Natural History and Geology. Nevertheless the museum will have a pivotal role in celebrations of the 150th anniversary of the founding of the Queen's Colleges in Ireland in 1995.

Principal collections:

The core of the museum is the type, figured and backup material for William King's Monograph of the Permian Fossils of England published by the Palaeontographical Society in 1850. The more spectacular mineral specimens belong to the recently acquired Eleanor Miles Collection. More recently a specific acquisition policy relating to material mainly from Atlantic Ireland has been established.

Archives:

King's original hand-written catalogues are still extant.

Number of specimens:
c. 15,000.

Published catalogues:

Pattison, J. 1977. Catalogue of type, figured and cited specimens in the King Collection of

The Eleanor Miles Mineral Collection

Permian fossils. *Bulletin of the Geological Survey of Great Britain*, **62**, 33-44.

Other publications:
Anderson, R.J. 1899. The Natural History Museum, Queen's College, Galway. *Irish Naturalists' Journal*, **8**, 125-131.

Feely, M. & Naughton, G. 1990. The Eleanor Miles Mineral Collection in the James Mitchell Museum, University College, Galway. *Annual Review of the Irish Association of Economic Geologists 1990*, 43-46.

Fewtrell, M.D. 1979. The James Mitchell Geology Museum, University College, Galway. *Irish Naturalists' Journal*, **19**, 309-310.

Fewtrell, M.D. & Ryan, P.D. 1979. Queen's College Museum, Galway. *Newsletter of the Geological Curators' Group*, **2**, 173-181.

Harper, D.A.T. 1988. 'The King of Queen's College': William King D.Sc., first professor of Geology at Galway. *In* D.A.T. Harper (ed.)

William King D.Sc. a palaeontological tribute, pp.1-24. Galway University Press.

Harper, D.A.T. 1992. The James Mitchell Museum - a museum of a museum in University College Galway. *Geological Curator*, **5**, 292-297.

King, W. 1850. Monograph of the Permian fossils of England. *Monograph of the Palaeontological Society*, 258 pp.

Displays:

New exhibitions featuring the more spectacular rock, mineral and fossil specimens together with the geological history of the west of Ireland and the life and times of William King were prepared for the reopening of the museum in 1992.

Public services:

The museum supports a full enquiry service. School and college parties are catered for with prior warning. Moreover the museum has an active role within most geological events in the west of Ireland, for example, Irish Geology Day, Adult Education classes and visiting conferences and fieldtrips.

Research facilities:

Accommodation, computing and microscope facilities are available in the geology department which is attached to the museum.

Current projects:

The museum has recently been refurbished with support from a FAS (An Foras Aiseanna Saothair) community response team which included two co-ordinators and a floating population of around 15 trainees. It was formally relaunched in November 1992 with additional aid from the Heritage Council. Restoration of the main gallery of the museum is in its original mid-19th century style. All museum material has now been curated and catalogued both manually and on a purpose-built computerised database. Finance is currently being sought to aid conservation of the more important specimens, for example, the Holzmaden ichthyosaur and the Lyme Regis plesiosaur.

Staff:

Honorary Keeper and Curator of the palaeontological collections, David A.T. Harper, BSc, ARSM, PhD, FGS, CGeol; Curator of the rock and mineral collections, Martin Feely, MSc, PhD, MIMM.

Compiler:

David A.T. Harper.

NORTH AND NORTH-WEST ENGLAND

BOLTON
Bolton Museum and Art Gallery

Address:
Le Mans Crescent, Bolton, BL1 1SE. Telephone 0204 22311, ext. 2211/2197.

Administration:
Bolton Metropolitan Borough.

Admission:
Free.

Times of opening:
Monday, Tuesday, Thursday, Friday 09.30 - 17.30, Saturday 10.00 - 17.00, Wednesday, Sunday closed.

History:
Founded 1883. Moved to present premises in 1930's.

Principal collections:
Rooke Pennington (1844-1887); James Lomax (1857-1934); John Starkie Gardner (1844-1930); Philip Brooks Mason (1842-1903); George R. Vine; Matthew Dawes (1804-1860).

Major strengths:
Coal Measure fossils.

Displays:
Minerals; local geology.

Staff:
Three Natural History curators, but no geologist on staff at present.

Compiler:
S.P. Garland.

NORTH AND NORTH-WEST ENGLAND

CARLISLE
Tullie House Museum and Art Gallery

Address:
Castle Street, Carlisle, CA3 8TP. Telephone 0228 34781; Fax 0228 810249.

Administration:
Carlisle City Council.

Admission:
Free to ground floor including Art Gallery. Upper floors as follows: Adults £3.30; senior citizens, children (under 16), registered unemployed, wives of unemployed, those on income support (including spouse), those on family credit (including spouse), registered disabled, YTS trainees, full time students £2.00; local residents with Tullie Card free. Admission tickets can be validated for 1 week from time of issue. Education rate: £1.20 per head.

Times of opening:
Monday - Saturday 10.00 - 17.00, Sunday 12.00 - 17.00. Closed Christmas Day.

History:
The collections of the Carlisle Philosophical Society were given to the City in 1872 and a city museum was established in 1877. The Museum and Art Gallery has operated from Tullie House since 1893 during which time it has undergone several expansions. The Museum has extensive Natural Science, Human History and Art collections.

Principal collections:
Collection of Professor R. Harkness (1816-1878), mainly British, includes a number of figured specimens. Harkness was Professor of Geology at Cork University (1853-1878) and did much pioneering work and published several papers on the geology of Cumbria and Scotland. Other contributors to the collections were J. Clifton-Ward, J.G. Goodchild, Miss J. Donald, A. Colvin and Lady Mabel Howard.

Major strengths:
Local rocks; minerals from Lake District and Pennines, including high quality material from Caldbeck Fells.

Geology Collection Storage

Number of specimens:
c. 6,000 fossils (including figured/referred Permian footprints); c. 1,000 rocks; c. 3,000 minerals.

Displays:
No permanent geology display. Temporary exhibitions of the collections will occur in both the charging and non-charging parts of the Museum.

Staff:
Keeper of Natural Sciences, Stephen Hewitt.

Compiler:
Stephen Hewitt.

NORTH AND NORTH-WEST ENGLAND
CLITHEROE
Clitheroe Castle Museum

Address:
Castle Hill, Clitheroe BB7 1BA. Telephone 0200 24635; Fax 0200 24635.

Administration:
Borough Council and County Council.

Admission:
Adults £1.00; over 60's £0.50; children free.

Times of opening:
Open everyday from Easter until end of October. April, October 11.00 - 16.30, May - September, Bank Holidays 11.00 - 17.00. Last entry half an hour before closing.

History:
The Museum is in the group of buildings on Castle Hill in Clitheroe. Apart from the Castle Keep, these include buildings that were formally the offices and the house of the Steward of Honour of Clitheroe. The Museum had a store and display room in the offices when it was founded in 1945. The collections were begun by local appeal, and contain a wide variety of social history, archaeology. ethnography, natural history and miscellanea, as is usual for a small town museum.

In 1980 the Museum took over the house when the Borough Council, who had been using it as their offices, moved into new premises and the County Museum Service was asked to take care of the collections and displays. Shortly afterwards the full-time geological post of Assistant Keeper was created within the service, and was based at Clitheroe. The Museum now houses the history collections for the Borough, and the geology collections for the County Museum Service. The ground floor is given to local history displays and the first floor to geology.

Principal collections:
Half of the total collection belong to the J. Ranson and D.H. Learoyd Collection. Smaller collections, mostly of local amateurs, include R. Fort; S. Westhead; J. Wright; D. Parkinson; G.M. Davis; A. Seedall; M. Sowden.

Lead mine reconstruction, Geology Gallery

Major strengths:
Wide ranging, but emphasis on Lower Carboniferous palaeontology of the surrounding area, particularly crinoid and brachiopod faunas of the Waulsortian build-ups of mud otherwise known as 'reef-knoll' limestones.

Number of specimens:
c. 25,000 (including 3 type, 3 figured).

Displays:
Five geology galleries including the following displays: *Roadside Geology:* which illustrates the geology along the main roads of the Ribble Valley.

The Salthill Trail: which looks at the well-known geological trail in a disused quarry.

The Mineral World: which displays mineral specimens from the collections including fluorescent varieties.

The Westhead Room: a brief look at the activities of some of the local amateur palaeontologists and which is a memorial to one of them.

More Than Just Rock: a look at the economic geology of the area. This is the largest and newest of the galleries, having been opened in mid-1990. It contains a greater variety of material than the older galleries, with life-size reconstructions, working models and audio-visual material.

Current projects:
Present work in the Museum, apart form the routine work on the collections, is now directed towards supplementing the galleries. Worksheets are planned for both floors of the

museum and hopefully, a set of education projects will be established in one of the rooms of the museum, providing half day or full day activities for school parties. A further room is to be given to temporary displays.

Staff:

Assistant Curator (Geology), Phillip Manning MSc, FAECT.

Compiler:

P. Manning.

NORTH AND NORTH-WEST ENGLAND
KENDAL
Kendal Museum

Address:
Station Road, Kendal, LA9 6BT. Telephone 0539 721374.

Administration:
The Lake District Art Gallery and Museum Trust on behalf of South Lakeland District Council.

Admission:
Adults £2.50; children, senior citizens, students £1.25; Museums Association members free.

Times of opening:
Summer hours: Monday - Saturday 10.30 - 17.00, Sunday 14.00 - 17.00; Shorter Winter opening hours.

History:

Founded 1913. The history of the Museum's collections can be traced back to one of the Lake District's earliest museums, Todhunter's Museum. William Todhunter set up his museum near Abbots Hall in 1797 and amongst its many curiosities were numerous geological specimens and sets of "musical stones". Following his death the contents of the museum were sold in 1835 and acquired by the Kendal Literary and Scientific Society, founded in the same year. The collections, in which geological specimens formed a prominent part, were displayed in the Society's museum in Lowther Street.

The first Hon. Curator, Dr Thomas Gough, together with Adam Sedgwick and John Ruthven, were mainly responsible for assembling the geological collection. Adam Sedgwick (1797-1876), a native of nearby Dent and one of Britain's greatest field geologists, became the Society's President in 1840 and greatly influenced its running for the next 30 years. It is not surprising that the collection was reputed to be one of the finest and most comprehensive in the country. The museum continued to grow and in 1854 moved to Stricklandgate House, a mansion formerly owned by the Maude family. The geological collection was displayed to illustrate the geology of the Kendal district.

In 1888 the Society purchased a number of post Pleistocene mammal bones, including a complete skeleton of a wolf, discovered in a fissure at Helsfell by John Beecham. The specimens were examined and assembled by Sir Richard Owen who was also a member of the Society.

Lake District Natural History Gallery

Although the collection had a local emphasis, it contained some fine quality material from other localities. Amongst these were a number of ichthyosaur specimens including a complete skeleton from the Oxford Clay of Peterborough originally part of the Leeds Collection. There was also a good selection of world-wide minerals. The collection also contained type and figured material.

Towards the end of the century the Society began to lose momentum and by 1910 had run into financial difficulties. Some of the collections were sold to the British Museum and the residue was presented to the Kendal Town Council to form the basis of a municipal museum; the Society was then wound up. In 1913 local benefactors, the Allen Trustees, purchased part of a redundant wool warehouse as the Kendal Borough Museum. The Museum was opened in 1918 and the extensive geological collection was displayed in the basement. The specimens were arranged by Canon George Crewdson, an enthusiastic and knowledgeable local amateur geologist, who had also contributed to the collection.

The Museum was administered by the Town Council through a succession of Hon. Curators. Interest in the geological collection gradually declined and by the end of the Second World War the collection was in a poor state. In 1958 following the recommendations of the Joint Committee of the Museums Association and the Carnegie United Kingdom Trust, it was decided to close the basement gallery and dispose of geological specimens. A large part of the collection, including most of the best specimens, were sold in the 1960's to Liverpool, Hull and Wigan

Museums. The ichthyosaur material, including the large skeleton, went to Hull Museum, but the latter is now in Scunthorpe Museum.

In 1974, following local government reorganisation, the museum passed into the ownership of South Lakelands District Council who, in 1977, placed its management into the hands of a private trust, the Lake District Art Gallery Trust. In 1978 a full time professional curator was appointed with the objective of creating new displays and collections to reflect Kendal and its surrounding region. In 1979 work commenced on the Lake District Natural History Gallery which was to include a geological display. The new gallery was opened to the public in 1981. Many of the specimens used in the gallery were kindly returned on loan by Merseyside Museum. The Museum won a special judges award in the Museum of the Year 1986.

Principal collections:

Today the collection is just a remnant of a once superb and historically important collection. Unfortunately it is not possible to recognise the individual nineteenth century collections of Gough, Sedgwick, Ruthven or Crewdson. Many specimens have their original numbers and identifications which refer to two catalogue books compiled by R. Bullen Newton in 1884-1885.

Archives:

Catalogues by R. Bullen Newton (see above), Official Handbook and Catalogue of the Kendal and Borough Museum 1924, Stock Book of the Lower Gallery of Kendal Borough Museum 1939-1940, Inventory of the Geological Collections 1991, correspondence particularly relating to the disposal of the geological collections, and photographs, press cuttings and other papers referring to the Museum and to Kendal Literary and Scientific Society. There is a small library containing rare nineteenth century geology books.

Major strengths:

Thanks partly to Merseyside Museum, the collections include a reasonable range of specimens from Kendal and the southern Lake District. The emphasis is on Palaeozoic fossils, particularly from the Silurian Ludlow rocks of Benson Knott and the Carboniferous Limestone of Kendal Fell. This material was collected almost entirely during the last century and although identified has little provenance detail.

The general collection contains examples of most fossil groups and has a wide stratigraphical range, mainly from Lake District and British localities. Amongst the vertebrate material are a few ichthyosaur specimens which are possibly part of the Leeds Collection. There is also a fine *Dapedius* from Barrow-on-Soar, Leicestershire, donated by Samuel Marshall, and some fine figured starfish.

Both the small rock and mineral collections contain a reasonable range of Lake District and Kendal samples. Much of this material was donated by Dr F.H. Day, a Cumbrian geologist, in 1982.

Number of specimens:

1,000 fossils, 400 rocks, 200 minerals.

Displays:

The Lake District Natural History Gallery on the first floor of the Museum starts with a geology display which illustrates the history of the area from 520 million years ago to the present day. Attractive reconstructions of past environments are viewed through circular windows which are surrounded by geological specimens. A mural of *Rocks and the Landscape* using photographs and handling specimens shows how the varied geology of the Lake District has influenced the scenery.

Public services:

Activities for the public and school parties with use of worksheets and good handling collection. Education area in Museum basement. Active children's Saturday club. Reserve collection may be viewed on request. Identification Service, Conservation Advisory Service.

Compiler:

Rosemary Roden.

NORTH AND NORTH-WEST ENGLAND
LIVERPOOL
Liverpool Museum

Address:
William Brown Street, Liverpool, L3 8EN. Telephone 051 207 0001; Fax 051 207 3759.

Administration:
National Museums and Galleries on Merseyside.

Admission:
Free.

Times of opening:
Monday - Saturday 10.00 - 17.00, Sunday 12.00 - 17.00. Closed Christmas Day, Boxing Day, New Year's Day, Good Friday.

History:

The Museum dates back to 1851 when the 13th Earl of Derby bequeathed his zoological collections to the Liverpool Town Council. The collections remained predominantly zoological until 1867 when Joseph Mayer, a Liverpool goldsmith, donated his archaeological and ceramics collection to the Museum, now housed in a new building in William Brown Street.

The collections continued to grow until the Second World War when the Museum was burned out during the Liverpool blitz of May 1941. All the material on display, and the greater part of the collections in store were destroyed. For the next 15 years Liverpool had no public Museum until one gallery was reopened in 1956. The main part of the Museum was rebuilt in two phases in the 1960's.

In 1974 the Museum became the Merseyside County Museum under the new metropolitan County Council. When the latter was abolished in 1986, the Museum became part of a new body, the National Museums and Galleries on Merseyside, financed by the Office of Arts and Libraries, and administered by a board of trustees.

Principal collections:

The pre-war geological collections were almost completely destroyed by fire when the Museum was bombed in May 1941. Only the following four pre-war collections in part survived the blitz: Henry Higgins - Coal Measure plants, including type, figured and referred material (1870); Thomas Austin - Carboniferous crinoids

The Natural History Centre

from Ireland, Britain and USA (1886); Edward Henry Stanley, 15th Earl of Derby - agates and other polished stones (1893); J. Wilfred Jackson - Pleistocene and Holocene molluscs, mainly British (1936).

All other material in the collections has been acquired since 1941: Charles Trelease - minerals, mainly British (1942); Grosvenor Museum, Chester - fossils, mainly British (1942); Kathleen Crosse - British and foreign fossils (1942); J. Wilfred Jackson - rocks and minerals (1942); Sir Hugo Rutherford - crystals and cut stones (1943); H. Willoughby Ellis - vertebrate fossils from Kent's Cavern, Torquay, polished Devonian corals from S Devon, general fossils, mainly British (1944); J. Wilfred Jackson - mainly Pleistocene cave fossils (1945); Henry Seymour - Irish rock types (1947); F. Gilbert Smith - amber (1948); Imperial Institute, London - Burmese minerals and gemstones (1950); Bethell Robinson - polished agates (1952); Prof. Campbell Brown - minerals (1952);Joseph Davies - rocks from North Wales (1953); J.K.P. Edwards - British Mesozoic fossils (1954); A.W. Stelfox - Pleistocene and Holocene molluscs (1956); Dr Blair Macauley - British Eocene and Oligocene fossils (1958); Kendal Museum - British fossils (1960); Horsham Museum, Sussex - Pleistocene vertebrates (1963); Philip Cambridge -Plio/Pleistocene fossils from Britian, Netherlands, Belgium and Germany (1965); A.E. Salisbury - Cenozoic fossils (1965); J. Wilfred Jackson - fossil cowrie shells (1967); Manx Museum, Douglas - Plio/Pleistocene fossils (1969); O. Wilson - Cornish rocks (1969); E.

Neaverson - Lower Carboniferous fossils from North Wales (1970); J.W. Kitchen - British fossils, mainly Plio/Pleistocene crags (1971); J. Wilfred Jackson - British Carboniferous fossils (1971); Cheltenham College, Cheltenham - general collection (1976); David Mundy - Carboniferous Limestone fossils (1976/7 & 1981/2); D.A. Rae - Glacial erratic pebbles (1977); John Ranson - botanical and geological slides (1977); Ronald Collier - British fossil vertebrates (1978); T.A. Jones - Pebbles from Bunter Pebble Bed (1979); Ralph Sutcliffe - minerals from NW England (1980); Wellcome Institute for the History of Medicine - general collection (1981); W.J. Lewis Abbott - Rough gemstones (1981); Richard Lucas - British rocks (1981); J. Wilfred Jackson - Holocene molluscs (1983); Valerie Duke - Brazilian minerals and gemstones (1984); University of Liverpool - igneous and metamorphic rocks (1984); Frederick Burke - trilobite collection (1984); N.F. McMillan - Holocene shells from Norway (1986); University of Liverpool - mineral collection (1986); University of Liverpool - fossil collection (1988); Lindsay Greenbank - northern England minerals (1991).

Major strengths:

The collections are reasonably comprehensive, but the loss of most of the pre-war material means that strong points are few. The fossil collections are extensive with marine Devonian and Lower Carboniferous well-represented as are Pleistocene and Holocene molluscs. Unusual specimens include an egg of the small dinosaur, *Protoceratops*, two *Aepyornis* eggs and a complete skeleton of *Megaceros giganteus*. In recent years the reserve collections of the Liverpool University Department of Earth Sciences have been transferred to the Museum.

Number of specimens:

c.30,000 fossils, c.11,000 minerals, c.6,250 rocks.

Publications:

The Earth before Man - a guide to the Geological Gallery published by the Museum.

The Invisible Dinosaur - produced to commemorate the 150th anniversary of the discovery in 1838 of *Chirotherium* footprints at Storeton, Wirral.

Displays:

The Natural History gallery, opened in 1974, includes geological displays with the main emphasis on palaeontology. The geological section of the gallery has been given the title *The Earth Before Man*. The initial displays deal with rocks and their formation, and fossils - their nature, formation and use in correlating successions. Twelve cases summarise the changes in the life of the different geological periods, and form an introductory bay to a tunnel where the displays highlight the main evolutionary advances throughout geological time.
Successive displays illustrate: trilobites, Silurian sea diorama, Silurian fossils, Devonian fish, the Coelacanth, Coal Forest diorama, Carboniferous plants, the formation of coal, the Age of Reptiles, Ichthyosaurs, Jurassic dinosaurs, Cretaceous dinosaurs, *Protoceratops* and dinosaur eggs, pterosaurs, *Archaeopteryx*, Mesozoic mammals, the Ice Age, Ice Age diorama, Ice Age animals, the evolution of man.

Large free-standing exhibits include the skeleton of a Giant Deer and casts of the skeleton of two dinosaurs: *Allosaurus* and *Camptosaurus*. A notable exhibit is an 11 foot (3.3m) long sandstone slab showing the footprints of the Merseyside "dinosaur" *Chirotherium*.

Two cases entitled *An A.B.C. of Minerals* are included in the displays outside the new Natural History Centre.

Education:

The Museum organises classes in geology at all levels from adult education to primary schools. The Museum Education Service runs training courses for teachers in projects for primary and secondary schools which make use of the gallery displays, handling trays of specimens and museum workbooks. Practical classes for GCSE geology are also run by the Education Service (using selected material from the reserve collections), but the curatorial staff normally assist with "A" level classes.

A number of WEA. classes make evening visits to the department for practical work, as do groups working for the Diploma of the Gemmological Association. Members of the departmental staff themselves give lecture courses for both WEA and University Continuing Education Department.

Staff:

Curator of Earth and Physical Sciences, Geoffrey R. Tresise, PhD, FGS; Curator of Palaeontology, post vacant; Assistant Curator, Wendy Simkiss, BA.

Other information:

The Natural History Centre. The conventional displays show only a minute part of the collections and are in no way representative of the reference collections as a whole. The Natural History Centre, opened in 1987, attempts to increase visitors awareness of the nature and extent of the reserve collections.

The Centre consists of two rooms. The larger is an Activity Room where specimens are made available for examination, either by handling or through the use of microscopes or specially modified video-cameras. The smaller room is the Collections Room which houses some 30 cabinets of specimens drawn from the reserve collections. For example there are three cabinets of fossils, four of minerals and two of rocks. A micro-computer linked to the collections data base provides information on the minerals in store.

A small team of demonstrators, supplemented by temporary staff employed at weekends and in school holidays, play a key role in providing information on the specimens and answering visitors' questions. The Centre is open to the public in the afternoons (Tuesday - Sunday) and can be used by pre-booked school groups in the mornings.

The department collects information on geological sites in Cheshire, Clwyd and Merseyside. Staff are actively involved with the Merseyside R.I.G.S. group and are assisting with the Cheshire R.I.G.S. scheme.

Compiler:

G. R. Tresise.

NORTH AND NORTH-WEST ENGLAND
MANCHESTER
The Manchester Museum

Address
The University, Oxford Road, Manchester, M13 9PL.
Telephone 061 275 2660; Fax 061 275 2676.

Administration:
The Manchester Museum is both a university and public museum, supervised by a Museum Committee which includes representatives of both the University and the city. The collections are the property of the University, but the City of Manchester made annual grants to the Museum from 1895 until 1974. In 1974 this funding was replaced by capital grants and a contribution to the running costs from the Greater Manchester Council, but on its disbandment in 1986 all costs were taken over by the University with the aid of Special Factor Funding from the Universities Funding Council (UFC). In 1991 the Geology Department was designated as a Major Collection Centre by the UFC as part of their Earth Sciences Review and as such also receives Special Factor Funding. It is one of eight departments in the Museum under the general administration of the Museum Director.

Admission:
Free.

Times of opening:
Monday - Saturday 10.00 - 17.00. Closed Good Friday, May Bank Holiday, Christmas Day, Boxing Day, New Years Day.

History:

The Manchester Museum was founded by Manchester Natural History Society in 1821. At an early stage the collections included geological specimens which after several moves were placed in a specially built Museum (now demolished) in the centre of the city in 1835. The Manchester Geological Society, later to be called the Manchester Geological and Mining Society, was formed in 1838 and also built up collections which in 1850 were merged with those of the Natural History Society. In 1867 the collections were accepted by the newly formed Owens College (later to become Manchester University) and in 1873 they were moved to new buildings on the site of the present University. The first block of the present Manchester Museum fronting Oxford Road was opened in 1888 and the geology collections housed on the ground floor. These two galleries, together forming the Stratigraphical Hall,

The Williamson Stigmaria, a Carboniferous tree from Bradford, Yorkshire

still retain a number of the original cases. Further extensions were made in 1912, where the original cases displaying geology remain on the ground floor, and in 1927, where more storage space was provided. In 1977 the Museum was once more extended into an adjacent University building where its geological offices and some store space are situated on the top floor. In 1991, on being designated a Major Collection Centre by the UFC, the Geology Department took over the basement of the 1977 extension where two large store rooms, a preparation laboratory and a research room have been added.

Principal collections:
Armstrong, A.L. (1879-1958); Barnes, J. (1855-1928) with Holroyd, W.F.; Binney, E.W. (1812-1881); Bird, C. (1843-1910); Birley, C. (1851-1907); Earwaker, J.P. (1849-1895) through Boddington, H. (1915); Bolton, H. (1863-1936); Bowman, J.E. (1785-1841); Braithwaite, R.S.W.; Bray, A. (fl.1920-1930); Broadhurst, F.M.; Brockbank, W. (1830-1896); Brown, T. (1785-1862); Buckman, S.S. (1860-1929); Cairns, R. (1854-1911); Cumberland, G. (1754-1848); Darbishire, R.D.(1826-1908); Dugdale, C. (fl.1850-1870); Dawkins, W.B. (1837-1929); Dawes, M. (1804-1860); Dixon, A. (fl.1880-1901); Eagar, R.M.C.; Forbes, D. (1828-1876); Gibson, S. (1790?-1849); Gregory, H.H. (1895-1950); Hadfield, G. (1787-1879); Harwood, H.F. (1886-1974); Heywood, J. (1810-1897); Hickling, H.G.A. (1883-1954); Holmes, F.A. (1871-1947); Holroyd, P.; Homfray, D. (1822-1893); Jackson, J.W. (1880-1978); Jones, D.G. (1927-1980); Kay-Shuttleworth, U.J. ((1844-1939); Lacey, W.S.; Lightbody, R. (d.1874); Manning, P. (coll. donated 1901); Miller, J.; Melville, J.C. (1845-1929); Moore, E.W.J.

(1887-1970); Nudds, J.R.; Ogle-Skan, J.F. (1921-1973); Owen, D.E. (1912-1987); Parker, T. (fl. 1870-1890); Parker, W.A. (1855-1918); Prince, W.D.; Roeder, C. (1848-1911); Royle, J.C. (1892-1955); Stirrup, M. (1831-1907); Stopes, M.C. (1880-1958); Strutt, J. (1765-1844); Sutcliffe, W.H. (1855-1913); Taverner-Smith, R.; Wagner, R.H.; Walton, J. (1895-1971); Waters, A.W. (1847-1929); Watson, D.M.S. (1886-1973); Wild, G. (1827-1903); Williamson, W.C. (1816-1895); Woodward, A.S. (1864-1944).

Archives:

Various, relating to above collections, especially A.L. Armstrong (notebooks); W.B. Dawkins (note books, diaries, correspondence, papers etc.); R.M.C. Eagar; J.W. Jackson.

Major strengths:

19th century palaeontological collections in classical localities in England, Wales and Scotland, with emphasis on Old Red Sandstone fishes; Lower Carboniferous plants; Lower Carboniferous and Namurian molluscs, Coal Measure (Westphalian) plants; non-marine bivalves and fishes from the north and north-west of England; Triassic footprints; Jurassic ammonites (Buckman Collection) and plants (Yorkshire and Sutherland); Pleistocene mammals (Dawkins, and Armstrong Collections, Creswell Crags); the Hicking Collection of coals and related rocks; non-marine bivalves from the Pennsylvanian of eastern USA and the Stephanian of north-west Spain; minerals from Cumberland, Derbyshire and Alderley Edge, Cheshire.

Number of specimens:

c.250,000 fossils, c.12,000 minerals, c.5,000 rocks; 631 type, c. 2,866 figured/referred.

Published catalogues:

Bolton, H. 1893. *Catalogue of the types and figured specimens in the Geological Department.* Manchester Museum.

Bolton, H. 1894. Supplementary list of type and figured specimens in the Geological Department, Manchester Museum, Owen's College. *Report of the Museums Association for 1894*, 250 - 254.

Jackson, J.W. 1952. *Catalogue of types and figured specimens in the Geological Department of the Manchester Museum.* Manchester Museum.

Nudds, J.R. 1992. Catalogue of type, figured and referred fossils in the Geological Department of the Manchester Museum. *Proceedings of the Yorkshire Geological Society*, **49**, 81-94.

Nudds, J.R. 1992. The R.M.C. Eagar Collection of non-marine bivalves; type and figured specimens in the Geological Department of the Manchester Museum. *Manchester Museum Publications New Series*, **NS.6.92**.

Other publications:

Eagar, R.M.C. & Preece, R. 1978. The Manchester Museum. *Geological Curators Group Newsletter*, **2**, 12-40.

Eagar, R.M.C. 1986. The Manchester Museum Geology Department. *Geology Today*, **2**, 182-183.

Displays:

The Stratigraphical Hall has a permanent display of British stratigraphy and palaeontology in two galleries which retain their original late Victorian (1888) design and atmosphere. They include a Carboniferous "Fossil Forest", with tree-casts of historic importance; the renowned mounted Williamson *Stigmaria* found in 1886 and later transported from Clayton, Bradford; and in the lower gallery exhibits dealing with the evolution of Tertiary mammals. The smaller Mineralogy Gallery, on the opposite side of Coupland Street, has displays of mineralogy, economic products of the north of England, Blue John and Derbyshire lapidary work, limestones and the work of water, local geology (extending into Derbyshire), coal and oil, and introductions to igneous and sedimentary rocks and to plate tectonics. There is a small geological garden to the north of the Museum, off Bridgeford Street, with emphasis on rocks of north-west England.

Public services:

The Department of Geology maintains a full enquiry service at all levels of academic and "public" scope. Access to the department library is available as part of this service, as is consultation of the reserve geological collections by bona fide research workers. Loans for scientific study are made world-wide on request.

Research facilities:

Computing facilities; trinocular, binocular and petrological microscopes; specimen photography; rock cutting and sectioning equipment. Also access to the University (John Rylands) Library and to the University Department of Geology which has full range of modern mineralogical and petrological analytical equipment.

Current projects:

Following the designation of the Geology Department as a Major Collection Centre by the UFC as part of their Earth Sciences Review, a complete rationalisation of storage is underway, removing all collections from the galleries to the new purpose built stores. Once completed it is hoped to embark on a major redisplay of all galleries.

Education:

The Museum Education Department has a suite of rooms in the basement of the Museum and provides both intra- and extra-mural teaching for local schools, colleges and educational establishments. All groups are requested to book their visits.

Staff:

Keeper of Geology, John R. Nudds, BSc, PhD, CGeol, FGS; Keeper of Mineralogy and Petrology, David I. Green, BSc, PhD; Cataloguer, Simon Riley, MSc.

Other information:

The University Department of Geology is situated in the Williamson Building on the opposite side of the Oxford Road from the Manchester Museum. Full research and library facilities are available where there are currently over 30 teaching staff in geology. The museum acts as the Geological Locality Records Centre for Greater Manchester and co-ordinates the local RIGS group.

Compilers:

J.R. Nudds & R.M.C. Eagar.

NORTH AND NORTH-WEST ENGLAND
MIDDLESBROUGH
Cleveland County Museum Service

Address:
Geology & Environmental Resources, Southlands Centre, Ormesby Road, Middlesbrough, TS3 0YZ. Tel. 0642 327583.

Administration:
Cleveland County Council.

Admission:
Free.

Times of opening:
By arrangement with the curator.

History:
The County Museum Service began life in 1973 with the creation of the new county of Cleveland from the old administrative area of Teesside. The county geological collection dates from 1975 and the appointment of the present curator. Specimens have been acquired mostly by purchase and field collection.

Principal collections:
R.W. Barstow; E. Simpson; Rev. J. Hawell; L. & P. Greenbank, incl. R. Sutcliffe. Further information in *A catalogue of Natural Science Collections in North-East England.*

Major strengths:
Mineralogy: important northern England material, especially north Pennines, Lake District and Caldbeck Fells. Many fine quality specimens from Teesdale and Weardale mines. General British and world reference collections as well as display material.

Macropalaeontology: main strength in regional and British Jurassic specimens including many plants from Marske Quarry; Durham Permian, especially fish; northern England Carboniferous, especially corals and brachiopods; Silurian Wenlock from Wales and Welsh borders.

Micropalaeontology: Durham Permian; Norwich Crag; Cromer Forest Beds; local Lower Jurassic; North Yorkshire Upper Oxford Clay; Durham Pleistocene.

Campylite on Psilomelane from Dry Gill Mine, Cumbria (CLEVE M5562, Ex Barstow Coll., Purchased by Prism Grant)

Number of specimens:
3,000 minerals, 4,000 macrofossils, 3,000 microfossils; 180 figured, 3 referred specimens.

Displays:
Small displays in the Margrove Heritage Centre, near Guisborough (admission free), telephone 0287 610368. Touring exhibitions.

Research facilities:
Extensive laboratory facilities including airbrasive equipment, fume cupboard, saw, lapping/polishing machines, binocular/trinocular and petrological microscopes, ultrasonic bath etc. Equipment available for use by arrangement with curator. Comprehensive library on local and regional geology, general reference works, *Palaeontology* and *Palaeontographical Society Monographs*. Microfiche. Identification service; Cleveland Site Records Centre; extensive collection of photographic slides; all collections on mainframe computer; indexes available free on request. Most mineral and fossil specimens recorded on colour slides.

Staff:
Environmental Resources Officer, Ken Sedman.

Compiler:
K. Sedman.

NORTH AND NORTH-WEST ENGLAND
NEWCASTLE-UPON-TYNE
The Hancock Museum

Address:
The University, Newcastle-upon-Tyne, NE2 4PT.
Telephone 091 2227418.

Administration:
Tyne and Wear Museum Service (from June 1992). Previously the University of Newcastle upon Tyne (from 1974) and originally The Natural History Society of Northumberland, Durham and Newcastle upon Tyne (founded 1829).

Admission:
Adults £1.50; children £0.75.

Times of opening:
Monday - Saturday 10.00 - 17.00, Sunday 14.00 - 17.00.

History:

Founded as the collections of Marmaduke Tunstall (1744-1790) of Welbeck Street, London. Tunstall Museum moved to Wycliffe on Tees, Yorkshire, 1780-1781; sold to George Allan (1736-1800) of Blackwell Grange, Darlington, 1791; opened to public 1792. Purchased by Newcastle Literary and Philosophical Society 1822 (whose collections had been growing since its foundation in 1793). Museum of the Natural History Society of Northumberland, Durham and Newcastle upon Tyne 1829. As Hancock Museum 1891. (For details see Goddard, T.R. 1929. *History of the Natural History Society of Northumberland, Durham and Newcastle upon Tyne (1829-1929).*

Principal collections:

T. Atthey (1814-1880); T.P Barkas (1819-1891); W. Dinning (fl.1860); J. Duff (fl.1870); J. Dunn (1865-1937); R. Howse (1820-1901); W. Hutton (1797-1860); J.W. Kirkby (1834-1902); A. Logan (b. 1937); Romonov Tsar Nicholas 1 (coll. 1830); T. Sopwith (1803-1897); T.S. Westoll (b. 1912); H.T.M. Witham (1779-1844); G.A. Lebour (1847-1918); A.G. Long (b. 1915); plus a further 500 collections.

"Yesterday's World"

Major strengths:

Carboniferous Coal Measure plants (W. Hutton and A.G. Long collections); Carboniferous vertebrates (T. Atthey collection); Permian and Carboniferous invertebrates (J.W. Kirkby and A. Logan collections); Permian fishes (W. Dinning collection).

Number of specimens:

c. 50,000 (including 230 type, 628 figured, 127 referred).

Published catalogues:

Boyd, M.J.F. and Turner, S. 1980. Carboniferous Amphibians. *Transactions of the Natural History Society of Northumbria*, **46**.

Howse, R. 1880. Fossil plants from the Hutton collection (presented by the Council for the Mining Institute to the Natural History Society, 1883). *Natural History Transactions of Northumberland, Durham and Newcastle upon Tyne*, **10**.

Newman, A. and Chatt-Ramsey, J. 1988. *A catalogue of specimens figured in the Fossil Flora by John Lindley (1799-1865) and William Hutton (1797-1860) held by the Hancock Museum, Newcastle upon Tyne, including a biography of William Hutton.* The Hancock Museum.

Displays:

Geological alphabet: designed primarily to introduce the layman to a limited number of specialist terms and to try and dispense with the jargon which can alienate the general public. A single geological term or concept is taken for each letter of the alphabet which is then explained briefly in terms of everyday experience.

Geology of Northumbria: a display which illustrates the geological origins of Northumberland together with an introduction to more general geological concepts. These range from the beginnings of the solar system to a brief explanation of ice ages. Displays also feature the work of Thomas Atthey, a local Victorian grocer whose passion for Coal Measure vertebrates established one of the most important collections held by the Hancock Museum.

Mineral Kingdon: this presentation starts with an introduction to mineralogy and petrology. Minerals and rocks are explained in terms of their uses to our industrial society. The display also concentrates on the aesthetic beauty of the specimens.

Fossil Kingdom: an exhibition to introduce palaeontology. It describes the processes by which fossils may be formed and through a series of topics seeks to explain the uses of fossils and what they tell us about our world.

Research facilities:

Access to the following may be arranged: microscopes; a range of photographic equipment, including dark rooms; X-ray diffraction and scanning electron microscope facilities. Also ultrasonic airbrasive, pneumatic development equipment, chemical extraction facilities, together with rock sawing, grinding and polishing equipment. A comprehensive range of maps including some early examples are available.

Current projects:

Rationalisation of storage areas, environmental control and extensive conservation work is being undertaken. The cataloguing of the collections is now well advanced with details of 40,000 specimens stored on the university mainframe computer. Changes in the operating system have required a reappraisal of the software and the data is now being converted to MODES. Geological site recording is progressing with details of 1,742 individual sites in Northumberland recorded on the computer. A series of published catalogues is planned using a new laser printer facility.

Staff:

Principal Keeper, Natural Sciences, A. Coles BSc, AMA, FLS; Assistant Keeper, Biology, E. Morton; Assistant Keeper, Geology, S.G. McLean, MSc.

Other information:

Other geological resources in close proximity include: British Geological Survey, Windsor Terrace, Newcastle upon Tyne (200 metres); The North of England Institute of Mining and Mechanical Engineers, Neville Hall, Westgate Road, Newcastle upon Tyne.

Compiler:

A. Newman.

NORTH AND NORTH-WEST ENGLAND

SUNDERLAND

Sunderland Museum and Art Gallery

Address:
Borough Road, Sunderland, SR1 1PP. Telephone 091 514 1235.

Administration:
Tyne and Wear Museums Service.

Admission:
Free.

Times of opening:
Tuesday - Friday 10.00 - 17.30, Saturday 10.00 - 16.00, Sunday 14.00 - 17.00. Closed all day Monday. Open Bank Holidays.

History:

Although the oldest recorded specimen dates back to 1815, the rest of the collection dates from 1836 when the Sunderland Natural History and Antiquarian Society was formed. Its collections passed into the care of Sunderland Corporation in 1846. Notable curators include the palaeontologist, William King (1809-1886), before his tenure as curator of the Hancock Museum, and the micropalaeontologist, J.W. Kirkby (1834-1901). In 1974, following Local Government Reorganisation, the administration of the museum was taken over by the Tyne & Wear County Council and became part of the Tyne & Wear County Museums Service. Geological collections from the Saltwell Towers Museum (Gateshead) and South Shields Museum were amalgamated with the Sunderland collections at this time. With the abolition of the County Council in 1986 the museum remained within a county wide framework funded jointly by the five Tyne & Wear Districts together with a grant from the Museums and Galleries Commission.

Principal collections:

Fossils and minerals from the UK and worldwide, collected by various benefactors in the 19th century.

Major strengths:

Comprehensive collection of mineral specimens from the North Pennine Orefield; Permian fossils, rocks and evaporites from the internationally famous outcrops of Zechstein strata in Tyne & Wear and County Durham, including the only British specimen of the Permian gliding reptile, *Coelurosauraus jaekeli* (Weigelt); Carboniferous plant and vertebrate fossils from the Durham and Northumberland Coal Fields; Jurassic invertebrate fossils from Cleveland and N Yorkshire.

Number of specimens:

c. 40,000; 2 types, c.20 figured/referred.

Displays:

An exhibition gallery entitled *Lost Worlds* illustrates the geological history of North-Eastern England with particular reference to the counties of Tyne & Wear and Durham.

Staff:

Keeper of Geology, S.G. McLean, MSc.

Compiler:

T.H. Pettigrew.

NORTH AND NORTH-WEST ENGLAND
WARRINGTON
Warrington Museum and Art Gallery

Address:
Bold Street, Warrington, Cheshire, WA1 1JG.
Telephone 0925 442391.

Administration:
Warrington Borough Council Community Services Directorate.

Admission:
Free. School parties must book in advance through the Museum Education Services Officers. (There is a charge for organised school visits.)

Times of opening:
Monday - Friday 10.00 - 17.30, Saturday 10.00 - 17.00. Closed Sundays and Bank Holidays.

History:
This public museum was established in 1848. It had as its nucleus the collections of the Warrington Natural History Society founded in 1838. The present building, opened in 1857, was primarily a museum, but in 1876, 1931 and 1990 Art Galleries were added. In 1936 the Geology Room was completely refurbished and redisplayed with the assistance of Carnegie UK.

Principal collections:
Ackerley (1849); C. Birley (1851-1907); P.P. Carpenter (1819-1877); G.A. Dunlop (1868-1933); B. Fairclough (1876-?); J. Peers (1838-1892); R. Pennington (1844-1887); T.G. Rylands (1818-1900); I.E. Taylor (1909); G. Thompson; E.J. Withington (1919); J. Robson (1928).

Major strengths:
Triassic slabs and footprints; world-wide minerals; Cardiff fossils; Pleistocene mammals from Derbyshire.

Number of specimens:
c. 9,250.

Displays:
The Geological Room is very much a period piece and retains its 1930's atmosphere with the emphasis on classification of fossils from the various geological periods. Over 1,000

Geology Gallery

specimens are on view including a selection of Triassic footprints including *Rhynchosaurus* and *Chirotherium*. Also some minerals and rocks.

Research facilities:
Binocular microscope, specimen photography, photocopying facilities, access to Warrington Libraries local history archive.

Staff:
Curator, Alan Leigh, BSc, AMA.

Compiler:
A. Leigh.

NORTH AND NORTH-WEST ENGLAND

WIGAN

Wigan and Leigh College Geology and Mining Museum

Address:
P.O. Box 53, Parsons Walk, Wigan, WN1 1RS.
Telephone 0942 501501; Fax 0942 820257.

Administration:
Wigan College of Technology.

Admission:
Free.

Times of opening:
During term: Monday - Friday 09.30 - 16.30.

History:

In 1858 the Wigan Mining and Mechanical School opened and geology was offered as a subject for examination. This created a focal point for geological specimens throughout the region. In July 1884 a Mr Stent of New York presented a collection of Silurian fossils and a collection of minerals from Canada, leading to the creation of a permanent display. In 1903 the Mining and Geology Department moved to a new building in Library Street and the new Geology Museum was able to expand. Many past students donated specimens from all over the world in addition to research material from staff. In 1926 Mr J. Spencer donated a significant collection of minerals and rocks. In 1930 Mr W. Stanley donated gold sand and heavy minerals from Uganda. In 1932 Professor J. Tennant donated a collection of minerals, rocks and fossils and in 1937 the Champion Reef Gold Mines of India Ltd. donated gold bearing rocks. In December 1946 the Manchester Geological Society moved its venue to the College and many specimens were absorbed into the collections over the next 25 years.

In 1959 the Department was transferred to the present location in the Parsons Walk Building and the museum was rehoused in a larger room. The teaching of Mining ended at the College in 1967, but the Geology Department survived and the expansion of the museum continued under I.A. Williamson, Senior Lecturer in Geology until 1980. In 1985/6 a demonstration

Diorama of Wigan in the Upper Carboniferous

area was created in the museum and in 1990 numerous materials of mining held in the College were finally put on display.

Principal collections:

Spencer Collection (1927) - Coal Measure fish and vertebrates; A.J. Tonge Hulton Shaft Collection (1911) -Hulton Colliery, Bolton, Chequerbent No. 1 Shaft Record; R.M. Chalmers Collection (1936) - Goniatites from Ravenhead Quarry, Upholland; I.A. Williamson Collection - Lake District material.

Archives:

Geological Map Reference Centre - total holding 3,300, includes total coverage of 1:50,000 and 1:25,000 for England and Wales, extensive coverage of County 6" Series for Lancashire, Victorian 6" and 1" vertical columns and sections, selection of "Dickinson" Lancashire maps, plus many other UK, Irish and overseas maps. Also large collection of regional geology books, plus general geology and some periodicals.

Major strengths:

Coal Measure material, especially Wigan Coalfield; Coal Measure tonsteins; general biostratigraphy; mining materials.

Number of specimens:

c. 19,000.

Publications:

Grayson, R.F. & Williamson, I.A. 1977. *Geological Routes around Wigan.* Wigan and District Geological Society.

Displays:

52 permanent displays including British stratigraphy, geology of the Lake District, geology of Shap, minerals of northern England, Solnhofen

fossils, Coal Measure biostratigraphy and Lomax Coal measure thin sections.

Staff:

Curators, Stephen Hewitt, BA, TCert; Roy Cash, MA, PGCE.

Compiler:

S. Hewitt.

YORKSHIRE AND HUMBERSIDE
DONCASTER
Doncaster Museum and Art Gallery

Address:
Chequer Road, Doncaster, DN1 2AE. Telephone 0302 734287; Fax 0302 735409.

Administration:
Doncaster Metropolitan Borough Council.

Admission:
Free.

Times of opening:
Monday - Saturday 10.00 - 17.00, Sunday 14.00 - 17.00.

Principal collections:

Henry Culpin; W.S. Bisat; E.E. Gregory; P.C. Buckland.

Major strengths:

Carboniferous fossils; world-wide minerals including many rare types. Post-glacial entomological sub-fossil collection.

Displays:

Cover all main aspects of geology.

Staff:

Keeper of Natural Sciences, Peter Skidmore.

Compiler:

Peter Skidmore.

YORKSHIRE AND HUMBERSIDE

HUDDERSFIELD
Tolson Memorial Museum

Address:
Ravensknowle Park, Wakefield Road, Huddersfield, HD5 8DJ. Telephone 0484 530591.

Administration:
Kirklees Metropolitan Council Cultural Services.

Admission:
Free.

Times of opening:
Monday - Friday 11.00 - 17.00, Saturday - Sunday 12.00 - 17.00; telephone for holiday arrangements.

History:
Originally a private residence, the building was given to the people of Huddersfield (as a museum) in 1922 by Legh Tolson in memory of his two nephews killed in the Great War.

Principal collections:
Learoyd Collection of minerals; Davis collection of Carboniferous fish fossils.

Major strengths:
Stored in three sections: minerals, rocks and fossils. The collections are strongest on local Carboniferous material, but the fossils are representative of Britain as a whole, and the minerals are world-wide in their provenance. The current acquisition policy limits additions to local material.

Number of specimens:
8,500 fossils, c. 3,000 minerals, 1,500 rocks.

Displays:
There are currently no natural history displays at the museum, but new galleries are being planned. Recent temporary exhibitions have included the *Tolson Rocky Road Show* (1992) aimed at children during the summer holidays, and included a Carboniferous diorama and an exhibition of dinosaur memorabilia.

Public services:
An enquiry service is maintained for the general public, students and professional geologists. Bona fide research workers are able to consult the collections.

Staff:
Senior Officer (Museums), J.H. Rumsby BA, AMA; Assistant Museums Officer (Natural History), C.S.V. Yeates, BA, AMA.

Compiler:
C. Yeates.

YORKSHIRE AND HUMBERSIDE
KEIGHLEY
Cliffe Castle Museum

Address:
Spring Gardens Lane, Keighley, BD20 6LH. Telephone 0535 618230; Fax 0535 610536.

Administration:
Bradford Metropolitan Council.

Admission:
Free.

Times of opening:
April - September: Tuesday - Sunday 10.00 -18.00; October - March: Tuesday - Sunday 10.00 - 17.00. Closed Mondays, Good Friday, Christmas Day. Open Bank Holiday Mondays.

History:
The present museum service began in 1974 with the formation of Bradford Metropolitan Council. The old collections of the former Councils of Keighley, Ilkley and Bradford were then amalgamated. These three public museums had been established in the 19th century, all of them acquiring private museum collections of local scientific societies, as well as building up acquisitions of their own.

Cliffe Castle, once a lavishly furnished house built in the 1870's opened as a museum in 1960 replacing the old Keighley Museum in Victoria Hall where natural sciences had always been strongly represented. Cliffe Castle now specialises in natural sciences and the District's geology collections and permanent displays are housed there.

Principal collections:
Bradford Philosophical Society (1865-c.1880); Joseph Dawson (1740-1813); John MacLansborough (pre 1900); Charles Croft (1836-1914); J. Spencer (pre c.1908);G.Campbell (pre 1906); John Holmes (1867-1945); James Ellison (pre 1891); and forty other named collections.

Major strengths:
Palaeozoic invertebrates; Upper Carboniferous plants.

Number of specimens:
c. 30,000; 2 types, 2 figured.

Reconstruction of Upper Carboniferous amphibian, Pholiderpeton, Airedale Gallery

Published catalogues:
Armstrong, A.C. 1979. City of Bradford Metropolitan Council Natural Sciences collections; part 2- geology. *Naturalist*, **104**, 17-23.

Hartley, M.M. *et al.* 1987. *Register of Natural Science collections in Yorkshire & Humberside*. Area Museum & Art Gallery Service for Yorkshire & Humberside.

Displays:
Airedale; the formation and life of a valley; specimens, models and photographs show how the area was moulded beginning with the cooling planet Earth, through the Carboniferous tropical swamps to the Ice Age.

Riches Underfoot; a fascinating collection of local products and old photographs shows how the mineral wealth of the area, lying on the edge of the Yorkshire Coalfield, has been exploited and utilised for centuries.

Molecules to Minerals; a thousand spectacular minerals explain what minerals are, how they are classified and how you can identify them from their fascinating physical properties. There's a chance to try out some properties for yourself.

Staff:
Senior Assistant Keeper Natural Sciences (Geology), Alison C. Armstrong BA, AMA.

Compiler:
A.C. Armstrong.

YORKSHIRE AND HUMBERSIDE
KINGSTON UPON HULL
Kingston upon Hull Museums and Art Galleries

Address:
Town Docks Museum, Queen Victoria Square, Hull, HU1 3DX. Telephone 0482 593902.

Admission:
Free.

Times of opening:
Monday - Saturday 10.00 - 17.00, Sunday 13.30 - 16.30.

History:

Hull City Museums had their origin in the collections formed by the local Literary and Philosophical Society during the nineteenth century. The Society's museum was opened on 15th July, 1823 and occupied two rooms at the Exchange; the first Curator was W.H. Dykes, FGS. From their beginnings the collections included important geological material; a series of Pleistocene mammal specimens from the Kirkdale Cave hyaena-den were among the first items presented to the museum. Moreover, William Smith and John Phillips are known to have presented fossils from the Yorkshire coast to the museum after their lectures to the Society in 1824.

By 1931 the size of the collections necessitated their removal to the Public Rooms on Jarrat Street where the museum occupied an upstairs room. The collections remained there until June 1855 when they were transferred to the newly completed Royal Institution in Albion Street. A guide to the museum published five years later reveals the existence of extensive geological exhibits, including fossils presented by Dr John Lee FRS (1783-1866) of Hartwell Park, near Aylesbury, and John Edward Lee (1808-1887) of Hull. Interestingly, the exhibits also included material of *Megaolosaurus* and *Iguanodon*, the first two dinosaurs to be scientifically described. Eventually the collections, whose maintenance were proving beyond the means of the Literary and Philosophical Society, were presented to Hull Corporation, who in 1900 appointed the energetic Thomas Sheppard FGS as Curator.

During the forty-one years of Sheppard's curatorship the geological collections were greatly enlarged and included some important palaeontological material. Tragically, however, the Central Museum in the Royal Institution was totally destroyed in an air-raid on 24th June 1943. The only significant geological survivals were part of the Mortimer collection of fossils, mostly from the Yorkshire Chalk, and a portion of the old Malton Museum collection (acquired by Hull in 1932), consisting of Oxfordian and Kimeridgian fossils from the Vale of Pickering.

At the time of writing (March 1992) it is apparent that material recovered from the site of the bombed Albion Street Museum by the Phoenix Project (set up in 1989 to excavate whatever might remain of the pre-war collections) includes approximately 10,000 geological specimens. To date, little of this material has been studied in detail, but it is clear that significant numbers of specimens from the 'lost' portions of the Mortimer and Malton collections are present.

Principal collections:

Mortimer, J.R. (1825-1911) - Upper Cretaceous fossils from North Humberside and North Yorkshire; Chadwick, Samuel (1845-1903) = Malton Museum - Upper Jurassic fossils from North Yorkshire; Parks, T.B. (1896-1961) - Jurassic and Cretaceous fossils from Lincolnshire, South Humberside and North Humberside; Fenton, Ken (1924-1985) - Jurassic, Cretaceous and Pleistocene fossils from North Humberside and North Yorkshire; Dunn, M.M. - Pleistocene mammals from North Humberside; Shillito, C.F.B. (1870-1950) - Holocene molluscs from Lincolnshire, Humberside and Yorkshire; Mason, C.W. (1884-1964) -Jurassic, Cretaceous and Pleistocene fossils from Humberside.

Major strengths:

Fossils from Upper Jurassic of Vale of Pickering, North Yorkshire and from Cretaceous and Pleistocene of North Humberside; glacial erratics from boulder-clays and gravels of Holderness.

Number of specimens:

c.12,000 fossils, c.1,500 rocks/minerals; 147 type/figured/referred. To this should be added c. 10,000 fossils, rocks and minerals recovered from the 'lost' pre-war collections.

Published catalogues:

Boyd, M.J. 1983. Catalogue of type, figured and cited fossils in Kingston upon Hull City Museums. *Geological Curator*, **3**, 476-485.

Other publications:

Edwards, C.R. 1983. Samuel Chadwick and the geological collections of the Malton Museum, North Yorkshire. *Geological Curator*, **3**, 496-505.

Edwards, P.L. 1984. The geological collections of Kingston upon Hull City Museums. *Geological Curator*, **4**, 19-28.

Staff:

Assistant Keeper of Natural History (Geology), Michael J. Boyd, MSc, MPhil.

Compiler:

Michael J. Boyd.

YORKSHIRE AND HUMBERSIDE
LEEDS
Leeds City Museum

Address:
Municipal Buildings, Leeds, LS1 3AA. Telephone 0532 478275.

Administration:
Leeds City Council.

Admission:
Free.

Times of opening:
Tuesday - Friday 09.30 - 17.30, Saturday 09.30 - 16.00. Closed Sunday, Monday and on some Tuesdays following Bank Holidays.

History:

The Museum was founded as the Museum of the Leeds Philosophical and Literary Society in 1821 and was transferred by agreement to the City of Leeds in 1921 to become the Leeds City Museum. The collections cover Natural Science, Archaeology, Ethnography, Geology and Numismatics.

The Society originally intended that the geology collection should illustrate the geology of the Leeds area and many of the early collections were derived from the Dales and the Yorkshire Coalfield. However, the scope was soon extended and specimens were accepted from outside Yorkshire. In 1822 a collection of North American fossils was acquired and in 1826 the Society purchased by subscription a number of Russian minerals, part of the collection of Sir Alexander Crichton, who was a physician to Tsar Alexander I. Over the succeeding years the collections were increased by donation, collection or purchase as the Curators tried to make them as comprehensive and wide ranging as possible.

In 1941 the Museum received a direct hit from an incendiary bomb which landed in the Natural History Section and in the chaos that followed specimens and records were separated and lost. As a result of this and previous re-accessioning, it is difficult to ascribe specimens to collectors or donors except in a few notable cases, e.g. a quartz crystal from the Crichton Collection.

Major strengths:
Good general collection which has strength in the range and quality of the specimens. There is a good range of Pleistocene material from British and foreign sites including numerous specimens with original field labels from the 1870's excavations at Kent's Cavern. Fossil plants from the Carboniferous and Jurassic rocks of Yorkshire are well represented.

Number of specimens:
c.20,000 fossils (including type, figured and referred), c.6,000 minerals, c.1,500 rocks, 500 thin sections.

Displays:
These are currently in preparation and will show general geological themes relating to local and regional topics.

Staff
Senior Curator, James H. Nunney.

Compiler:
J. H. Nunney.

YORKSHIRE AND HUMBERSIDE
SCUNTHORPE
Scunthorpe Museum and Art Gallery

Address:
Oswald Road, Scunthorpe, DN15 7BD. Telephone 0724 843533/280444, ext. 864; Fax 0724 280705; Telex 527733.

Admission:
Free.

Times of opening:
Monday - Saturday 10.00 - 17.00, Sunday 14.00 - 17.00.

History:

Founded in 1909 by three amateur geologists (Rev. S. Cutts, A. Dalton, H.E. Dudley), and one professional geologist (A.M. Cobban), under the auspices of Scunthorpe Naturalists and Antiquarian Society. Adopted by Scunthorpe Urban District Council in 1911. H.E. Dudley was Curator from 1913 to 1956. Except for a short period in its history the Museum has employed a geologist.

Principal collections:

Harold E. Dudley - large collection of local, mainly Lower Jurassic fossils; Canon John E. Cross - 177 local Lower and Middle Jurassic fossils including some type and figured specimens; Alexander M. Cobban - collection of local fossils, rocks and core samples; Rev. Samuel Cutts - local fossils; George V. Standerline - minerals; Adeline L. Sich - over 500 fossils and minerals, mainly from Gloucestershire and Yorkshire; Selby Museum - French rocks; David Stephenson - rocks; John Keen - Mesozoic reptiles; material from Hancock Museum, Tunbridge Wells Museum and Portsmouth Technical College obtained by exchange.

Major strengths:

Jurassic fossils from South Humberside and North Lincolnshire particularly Frodingham Ironstone ammonites, asteroids and crinoids..

Number of specimens:

8,000-10,000; 5 types, 3 figured, 7 referred.

Isocrinus robustus *from the Frodingham Ironstone*

Publications:

Knell, S.J. 1988. *The Natural History of the Frodingham Ironstone*. Scunthorpe Museum.

Displays:

Messengers from Paradise - a major gallery of local palaeontology and wildlife opened in April 1992. This includes a "Pepper's Ghost", a computer game, a satellite monitor and models. Parts of the Canon Cross Collection are on display in a Victorian parlour. The museum holds occasional temporary Geology displays.

Staff:

Keeper of Natural Sciences (Geology), Stephen Thompson, BSc; Natural Science Assistant (Geology) Sue Rainton.

Other information:

Geological Locality Records Centre for North Lincolnshire and South Humberside; regular activities particularly during the summer months; geological excursions for booked parties on request.

Compiler:

Simon J Knell.

YORKSHIRE AND HUMBERSIDE
SHEFFIELD
Sheffield City Museum

Address:
Weston Park, Sheffield, S10 2TP. Telephone 0742 768588.

Administration:
Sheffield City Council, Leisure and Tourism Services Programme Committee.

Admission:
Free.

Times of opening:
Tuesday - Saturday 10.00 - 17.00, Sunday 11.00 - 17.00. Closed Christmas Eve, Christmas Day, Boxing Day.

History:
Sheffield City Museum was founded at Weston Hall in 1875 when collections that had accumulated over the previous 50 years under the auspices of the Sheffield Literary and Philosophical Society were taken into the care of the local council. Much geological material was included in these early collections. In 1935 Weston Hall was demolished to make way for a new, purpose-built museum with five principal galleries.

Principal collections:
W.R. Barker - Coal Measure plant fossils (1963); Rev. J.M. Mello - Pleistocene mammals (1875); G.R. Vine - fossil bryozoans (1936); T. Bateman - Lower Carboniferous fossils (1893); Rev. Urban Smith - Lower Carboniferous fossils (1888); Col. J.W. Rimmington - world-wide minerals (1891-92); E.F. Newton - Cornish minerals (1895); J.W. Puttrell - Derbyshire minerals (1908 & 1939). A comprehensive listing can be found in Hartley, M.M. *et al.* 1987, *Register of Natural Science Collections in Yorkshire & Humberside*.

Major strengths:
Coal Measure flora of South Yorkshire (including coal ball thin sections); Pleistocene mammals of Derbyshire; Lower Carboniferous fauna of Derbyshire; minerals from South Pennine Orefield.

Number of specimens:
c. 20,000 fossils (including type material), c. 5,000 minerals/rocks.

Green fluorite from Cumbria

Published catalogues:
Riley, T.H. 1974. Type specimens in the palaeontological collections of Shefffiled City Museums. *Newsletter of the Geological Curator's Group*, **1**, 36-37.

Other publications:
Riley, T.H. & Torrens, H. 1980. Collections and collectors of note: White Watson (1760-1835). *The Geological Curator*, **2**, 573-577. Hartley, M.M. *et al.* 1987, Register of Natural Science Collections in Yorkshire & Humberside.

Displays:
Geology is concentrated within the Evolution Gallery, opened in 1976, and introduced through integrated displays highlighting the formation and evolution of the Earth, the genesis and composition of rocks and minerals, and the evolution of the main plant and animal groups. Displays of local geology concentrate on the changing palaeogeography of the Sheffield area throughout geological time and are supplemented by local rocks, fossils and minerals including Derbyshire Blue John and local Coal Measure tree fossils.

Public services:
Activities for the public include occasional special sessions and field excursions in addition to the established enquiry and identification service. The Education Section of the museum is able to provide geological talks for schools and other groups.

Research facilities:

Geology library including local geological maps, Geological Survey memoirs and Palaeontographical Society Monographs. Photocopying facilities available. Natural Sciences conservation/preparation laboratory. Shared museum photographic laboratory.

Current projects:

Computerisation of geological collections; strengthening collections of local Coal Measure plant fossils and South Yorkshire minerals.

Staff:

Assistant Keeper Meteorology/Earth Sciences, Gaynor Boon, MSc.

Other information:

Other geological resources in close proximity include the University of Sheffield Department of Earth Sciences, and the Sorby Natural History Society's Geological Section.

Compiler:

G. Boon.

YORKSHIRE AND HUMBERSIDE
SKIPTON
Craven Museum

Address:
Town Hall, High Street, Skipton, BD23 1AH.
Telephone 0756 794079.

Administration:
Craven District Council, Estates and Leisure Services Committee.

Admission:
Free.

Times of opening:
April - September: Monday, Wednesday - Friday 10.00 - 17.00, Saturday 10.00 - 12.00, 13.00 - 17.00, Sunday 14.00 - 17.00; October - March: Monday, Wednesday - Friday 13.30 - 17.00, Saturday 10.00 - 12.00, 13.30 - 16.30, Sunday closed.

History:
The museum began in 1928 as the private museum of the Craven Museum and Archaeological Society. It was offered to the then Skipton Urban District Council and was taken over by them on April 1st 1934. The town's librarian became the curator. The collections were housed at that time on the top floor of the public library building in the High Street. During the late 1950's and early 1960's, the museum was moved down to the ground floor and basement of the library and completely redisplayed. The first professional curator was appointed in 1972. In 1973 the museum moved to its present premises, a purpose-built annexe to the Town hall. In 1974 it was taken over by the newly-formed Craven District Council.

Principal collections:
R.H. Tiddeman Collection of Carboniferous Limestone Fossils, collected between 1890 and 1900 in the district between Pateley Bridge and Settle (on loan from the Craven Naturalist and Scientific Association); Munn Rankin Collection of glass slides of mountain limestone.

Major strengths:
Collections of Craven and northern England minerals and fossils, plus a few samples of local rocks.

Number of specimens:
c.17,500 (of which 15,000 are Tiddeman Coll.).

Lead ore crusher

Displays:
Silica and silicates, Minerals for Industry, Fossils and minerals from Craven.

Research facilities:
Researchers are welcome, but there is no study room. Appointment necessary.

Staff:
District Museums Officer, S.B. Kirrane, MA, AMA.

Compiler:
P.J. Mansergh.

YORKSHIRE AND HUMBERSIDE
WHITBY
Whitby Museum

Address:
Pannett Park, Whitby, YO21 1RE. Telephone 0947 602908.

Administration:
The Whitby Literary and Philosophical Society.

Admission:
Adults (including senior citizens and students) £1.00; children £0.50; party rates for schools only (per child) £0.25; teachers (ratio of 1 per 10 children £0.25. Schools <u>must</u> book visits in advance to avoid overcrowding.

Times of opening:
May - September: Weekdays 09.00 - 17.30, Sunday 14.00 - 17.00; October - April: Monday, Tuesday 10.30 - 13.00, Wednesday, Saturday 10.30 - 16.00, Sunday 14.00 - 16.00; Bank Holidays: Easter Friday, Saturday, Monday 10.30 - 16.00, Easter Sunday 14.00 - 16.00, Spring and Summer bank holiday Mondays 09.30 - 17.30. Closed Christmas Day, Boxing Day and New Years Day. It is advisable to phone beforehand if intending to visit btween Boxing Day and New Year's Day.

History:
Founded in 1823 as the Museum of the Whitby Literary and Philosophical Society in two first floor rooms at the harbour end of Baxtergate, Whitby. Relocated in 1827 in a purpose-built "Whitby Public Baths, Library and Museum Building", occupying the top floor, on the quayside. In 1931 the new Museum and Art Gallery was opened in Pannett Park which underwent major reorganisation in 1946.

Principal collections:
The museum's collection policy confines collections to material from within a twenty mile radius of Whitby, but being situated in the finest and most accessible exposures of Liassic strata in the British Isles, together with the industrial exploitation of the Alum Shales and the world renowned Whitby Jet industry of the last century, the collection displays the whole range of fauna from *Teleosaurus chapmani*, plesiosaurs, ichthyosaurs, an abundance of ammonites and belemnites together with fish and other marine fossils.

The coals, shales and sandstones of the Inferior Oolite Series have provided a rich coal plant fauna which is also well represented. More recently the development and working of the Boulby Potash Mine has provided an array of Zechstein evaporites which is being constantly added to.

The basis of the museum collection in its early days came from purchases locally, from local dealers such as Brown Marshall and from alum and jet workers. Martin Simpson was an assiduous collector and recorder and, many of his specimens are in the collection. Donations have been made over the years such as the *Ichthyosaurus platyodon* specimen found at Loftus alum quarry and donated by the Ripley brothers in 1847.

Archives:
All monographs, books and pamphlets are held in the Society library. There is a comprehensive collection of journals and a fine range of monographs relating to Jurassic fossils. Access to this material is by prior written application to the Honorary Librarian at the Museum.

Major strengths:
A large collection (arranged by family and stratigraphically) of ammonites and belemnites from the Whitby district; the wall-mounted saurians; the Zechstein evaporites from Boulby Mine.

Number of specimens:
Over 6,000 including many holotypes and neotypes.

Displays:
The saurians are permanently displayed on the south and east walls. There are cases exhibiting a fine range of ammonites, some belemnites, Jurassic coal plants, Zechstein evaporites and glacial erratics.

Public services:
The Museum provides a limited identification service for small specimens handed in and the Honorary Curator is available in the evening for telephone enquiries, preferably after 18.00 hours (0947 605676).

Staff:
Honorary Sectional Curator, Peter J. Thornton.

Compiler:
P.J. Thornton.

YORKSHIRE AND HUMBERSIDE
YORK
Yorkshire Museum

Address:
Museum Gardens, York, YO1 2DR. Telephone 0904 629745; Fax 0904 651221.

Administration:
North Yorkshire County Council.

Admission:
Adults £3.00 [£5.00]; students (with card), children, senior citizens, unemployed (with UB40) £1.75 [£3.00]; family rate (2 adults, 2 children) £7.00 [£12.00]; children under 5 free. Season ticket prices/annum are given in []. Party rates available on request. The charges are those applied when the museum has a major exhibition on show. Lower rates apply at other times.

Times of opening:
November 1st - March 31st: Monday - Saturday 10.00 -17.00, Sunday 13.00 - 17.00; April 1st - October 31st: Daily 10.00 - 17.00. Closed December 25th-26th and New Year's Day. Last admissions 16.30.

History:

1823 - founded as the museum of the Yorkshire Philosophical Society in Low Ousegate, York.

1831 - the museum moved to a purpose built building in the Museum Gardens.

1961 - Museum Gardens, buildings, collections etc. handed over to York City Council by the Yorkshire Philosophical Society.

1974 - Under local government reorganisation the North Yorkshire County Council took over the running of the Museum and Gardens which are constituted as a Charitable Trust (No 529710) under the Charitable Trusts Act 1853-1925. The Philosophical Society and City Council retained voting rights in the controlling committees.

Principal collections:

There are over 200 collections, mostly dating from the 19th century. Amongst them, many important Victorian collectors are represented. William Reed presented some 60,000 specimens drawn from various major collections. Examples include The Whincopp and Baker Collections of Red Crag material, the E. Wood Collection of Carboniferous fossils, and the Elwes Collection of Hampshire Tertiary material. These collections often contained type and figured material. Part of the William Bean

Collection was purchased (1859) and additional specimens came from John Leckenby via William Reed at a later date. Amongst the 5,000 specimens purchased are those figured by John Phillips and by Young and Bird. Other collections and specimens came from John Bainbridge (Yorkshire material in 1861), J.F. Walker (donations between 1863 and 1907), T.P Barkas (Northumberland Coal Measure fish remains in 1868), James Cook (Pleistocene vertebrates in 1872), the W. Horne Collection (1879) amongst which are fish teeth figured by Davies, and the Herries Collection (Yorkshire Jurassic in 1939) which has yielded a specimen figured by Wilfred Hudleston.

Archives:

William Reed provided the core of a fine geological library. While particularly well endowed with literature on Yorkshire, the library is wide ranging and provides a valuable resource for staff and researchers. The staff endeavour to maintain an up-to-date reference collection and would welcome offprints especially on Yorkshire and Northen England.

The Tempest Anderson Collection of c. 5,000 negatives of world-wide vulcanological topics (1880-1913) is of international importance.

Major strengths:

The Yorkshire Museum contains a wealth of invertebrates and vertebrate palaeontological material collected in the 19th century which together with the collection's great stratigraphic range provides a significant record of the collecting sites then available in the United Kingdom, many of them now extinct.

Number of specimens:

c.120,000; 1011 status specimens (this includes those which should be in the collection, but are at present unrecognised).

Published catalogues:

Pyrah, B.J. 1976-79. Catalogue of type and figured fossils in the Yorkshire Museum. *Proceedings of the Yorkshire Geological Society*, **41**, 35-47, 241-260, 437-460, **42**, 415-437.

Other publications:

Pyrah, B.J. 1988. *The history of the Yorkshire Museum and its geological collections.* Ebor Press, York.

Displays:

The first phase of a suite of new geology galleries, *Time Club,* was opened in January 1993.

Public services:

The Museum runs a geological enquiry service.

Staff:

Keeper of Geology, Paul C. Ensom, BSc, FGS, AMA; Senior Museum Assistant, Stuart Ogilvy, BSc.

Compiler:

Paul C. Ensom.

MIDLANDS
BIRMINGHAM
Birmingham Museum and Art Gallery

Address:
Chamberlain Square, Birmingham, B3 3DH.
Telephone 021 235 2929; Fax 021 236 6227.

Administration:
Birmingham City Council.

Admission:
Free.

Times of opening:
Monday - Saturday 11.00 - 17.00, Sunday 11.00 - 17.30.

History:
Natural History Museum founded 1913.

Principal collections:
Fossils, minerals, gemstones, rocks.

Major strengths:
Palaeozoic stratigraphy, Jurassic (oolite); Midlands geology; gemstones (second largest collection in British Isles).

Number of specimens:
5,000 gemstones, 5,000 minerals, 5,000 other.

Publications:
By the gains of industry; Birmingham Museums and Art Gallery 1885-1985. Birmingham Museums and Art Gallery publication.

Displays:
Triceratops prorsus skull and jaws; Quarter scale model of *Triceratops* with reproduction of painting of same by Eleanor M. Kish (Canadian Museum of Nature); *Tyrannosaurus rex* model (full size) and replica skull and jaws; Giant Irish Deer skeleton; Ichthyosaur skull and forelimb from Shipston-on-Stour (1955); Megalosaur bones from Cotswolds; reconstruction of *Titanites anguiformis* based on fossil from Worth Matravers; Half scale model of *Pteranodon* in flying pose; *Ichthyosaurus intermedius* skeleton; *Paradoxides* – giant trilobite.

Triceratops *skull from the central USA*

Staff:
Dr. R.J. Kennedy, Keeper of Natural History.

Compiler:
D.R.G. Walker.

MIDLANDS
BUXTON
Buxton Museum and Art Gallery

Address:
Terrace Road, Buxton, SK17 6DJ Telephone 0298 24658.

Administration:
Derbyshire County Coucil.

Admission:
Free.

Times of opening:
Tuesday - Friday 09.30 - 17.30, Saturday, Sunday 09.30 - 17.00. Closed Monday.

History:

The Museum was founded in 1891 by the Buxton Local Board and housed in the Town Hall. In 1928 it was relocated to its present building in Terrace Road, owned by the Borough. Derbyshire County Council took over the administration of the Museum from High Peak Borough when it was transferred in 1968. The Art Gallery was added to the museum in 1979 and has held a programme of short exhibitions of local and national artists since then. The *Wonders of the Peak* Gallery was opened in 1985 and shows the history of Buxton from earliest times to the present day.

Principal collections:

The J.W. Jackson Collection of Quaternary and Carboniferous fossils plus a large collection of papers (around 40,000 items) was donated in 1982.

The museum also holds good collections of both Ashford Black Marble and Blue John ornaments and items. The working of both these minerals is an industry unique to the Peak District.

Archives:

Sir William Boyd Dawkins, mentor and colleague of Jackson, opened the museum on its present site in 1928 and bequeathed his scientific papers and library to the museum.

There is also a large collection of local history items relating principally to Buxton, namely printed ephemera, photographs and miscellaneous bygones.

The Boyd Dawkins Room

Major strengths:

The geological collections are particularly strong in Carboniferous and Pleistocene specimens. The Quaternary mammal collection is very extensive and relates almost exclusively to the Peak District. The Dawkins and Jackson papers cover areas of cave palaeontology and pre-history and are of international significance.

Number of specimens:

20,000 Carboniferous fossils, 15,000 Quaternary mammals, 1,000 other fossils, 2,500 minerals, 2,000 rocks, 40,000 items in Jackson/Boyd Dawkins collections/archives.

Publications:

Bishop, M.J. (Ed.) 1982. *The Cave Hunters*. Derbyshire Museum Service. 48pp.

Displays:

The Wonders of the Peak, incorporating geological and palaeontological displays, dioramas and sets. Prehistory to present.

Staff:

Curator, Dorothy Harding.

Compiler:

D. Harding.

MIDLANDS
DERBY
Derby City Museum and Art Gallery

Address:
The Strand, Derby, DE1 1BS. Telephone 0332 293111.

Administration:
Derby City Council.

Admission:
Free.

Times of opening:
Monday 11.00 - 17.00, Tuesday - Saturday 10.00 - 17.00, Sunday 14.00 - 17.00.

History:

Derby City Museum has its origins in the Derby Town and County Museum and Natural History Society, founded in 1836. In 1858 the institution merged with the Derby Philosophical Society which supplied further specimens including many "fossils" and an extensive library. In 1870 the Museum was transferred to the ownership of Derby Corporation and in 1879 was moved to a new purpose-built building, extended both before the First War and in the early 1960's.

During the early years an extensive geological collection built up. However, up to 1949 much material was loaned at various times to local schools and colleges and has seemingly vanished without trace. In 1932 a disastrous flood in the Museum basement caused the loss of hundreds of geological specimens stored there, although it is not known exactly what was lost. The collections do not therefore do justice to a county noted for its geological riches.

Principal collections:

The present holdings include a number of significant collections. Among the most interesting are six inlaid tablets attributed to White Watson of Bakewell (1760-1835), showing cross-sections of strata. These include a section across Derbyshire from east to west, one of the few specimens to be rescued from the 1932 flood and showing signs of the resulting damage. There is an extensive series of Quaternary mammal remains from Creswell Crags, including part of a collection made by Thomas Heath, Curator from 1873 to 1883. There are also collections of Ipswichian interglacial material from

"On the Rocks" – part of the Derbyshire Nature Gallery

the vicinity of Derby including a spectacular and near complete *Hippopotamus*, excavated in 1895, and a variety of mammals excavated in 1972 from a sewer construction. Recent acquisitions include large and superb crystals of Matlockite and Phosgenite from Bage Mine, Cronford.

Number of specimens:

4,500 fossils, 2,500 minerals, 1,500 rocks; no status specimens.

Publications:

Stanley, M.F. 1976. Geological collections and collectors of note - Derby Museums and Art Gallery. *Geological Curators Group Newsletter*, **1**, 392-409.

Displays:

In 1991 a new gallery portraying the geology of Derbyshire was opened as the first phase of a Derbyshire Nature Gallery. This provides "hands-on" experience and a "time tunnel" in which a series of dioramas portrays Derbyshire at various episodes in the geological past. The relationship between geology and the landscapes of the County is strongly presented. The geological theme is to be carried on into the subsequent wildlife section (at present under construction) where the influence of the underlying rocks on habitats is stressed. The aim has been to create a visually stimulating exhibition to excite the ordinary visitor.

Staff:

Keeper of Natural History, William M. Grange; Assistant Keeper of Natural History, Nicholas J. Moyes.

Other information:

Geological Locality Records Centre for Derbyshire.

Compiler:

W. M. Grange.

MIDLANDS
DUDLEY
Dudley Museum and Art Gallery

Address:
St James's Road, Dudley, DY1 1HU. Telephone 0384 453571/4.

Administration:
Dudley Metropolitan Borough Council, formerly County Borough of Dudley (from 1903). Previously under the trusteeship of the Dudley and Midland Geological and Scientific Society and Field Club (founded 1862). Initially administered by Dudley and Midland Geological Society (founded 1842).

Admission:
Free.

Times of opening:
Monday - Saturday 10.00 - 17.00.

History:

The original collection was established by the Dudley and Midland Geological Society on its inauguration in 1842. One of the principle aims of this Society was the creation of a museum to house a complete series of fossils and rocks from the surrounding region. The initial impetus for this was a field visit of the British Association to Dudley in 1839 when several large private collections of fossils derived from the local Wenlock Limestone and Coal Measures were put on display. Selected material from these collections formed the core of the Society's collection which was housed and displayed in premises known as the Britannia Inn, situated near the centre of Dudley.

With a regular supply of quality fossils from the nearby mines and quarries the museum acquired a formidable reputation. However, the inexplicable demise of the Society during the 1850's resulted in closure and storage of the collections in an old malthouse.

In 1862 a new Society, the Dudley and Midland Geological and Scientific Society and Field Club was formed and acquired trusteeship of the collection which it rehoused in a Museum in the new Mechanics Institution building which was partly funded by the Earl of Dudley.

During the early years of the Field Club several collections were purchased from members for the Museum, but in 1901 the Club was discon-

Calymene blumenbachii – *commonly known as the "Dudley locust" or the "Dudley bug" from the local Wenlock Limestone*

tinued. The large collection that remained was handed over by the trustees to Dudley Town Council which rehoused it in the present museum. It was opened to public view in 1912 and a temporary curator, E.H. Worsey, was appointed to catalogue it.

During the Second World War the collection was transferred to Dudley Technical College, but subsequently moved back to the Museum where it remained in storage until 1965 when many of the best specimens were put on display in the present Geological Gallery. The bulk of the collection remained in the Museum basement until 1983 when it was partially rehoused and catalogued under a MSC scheme.

The first permanent curator in the collection's history was appointed in 1987 since when improved storage and cataloguing facilities have been introduced.

Principal collections:

No comprehensive Accession Register exists for either of the 19th century museums, merely a small Loans Collection Book dated 1865, with little information on the provenance of each specimen. An Accession Register was prepared by E.H. Worsey in 1912, once the collection had passed into Dudley's possession, but as Worsey had little documentation to hand, his register contains very little acquisition, locality or stratigraphical information.

A short list of donations to the first museum is given in the *Proceedings* of the original Society for 1842, but this unfortunately only alludes to the general type of material given by each donor and gives no idea of the quantity. Among the donors were John Gray and Charles Twamley, Honorary Curators of the first museum and the co-founders of the Society. Other donors from the Society included Cornelius Cartwright, Professor Henry Beckett, Samuel H. Blackwell and Francis Downing. Non-members who donated material included several well known collectors, notably Rev. T.T. Lewis and Lady Gordon Cumming. There is no reason to suppose that donated material was ever removed from the first museum by its original owners, but only a few items belonging to each of the above can now be traced.

According to the *Transactions* of the Field Club, a number of important collections of local material were purchased during the 1860's. These included the L.P. Capewell Collection (1866) and James Mushen and Charles Ketley collections (1867-1868). Nine Capewell specimens are known to exist in the present collection (including six figured fossils from the local Wenlock Limestone and Coal Measures). A similar number of Mushen fossils (mainly trilobites) are also present, while only two Ketley specimens have been traced.

While the above collections are probably extant at Dudley, there is no way to determine original ownership. Prominant members of both the original Society and the later Field Club amassed large private collections of local fossil material which they occasionally exhibited at Dudley, although the majority of these now reside elsewhere. The most important of these collections include: John Gray, Henry Johnson, James Mushen, Samuel Allport and William Madeley collections (now at The Natural History Museum, London); Charles Holcroft, Charles Ketley and Francis Downing collections (now housed at Lapworth Museum, Birmingham University); Captain Thomas W. Fletcher Collection (now at Sedgwick Museum, Cambridge); Eliot Hollier Collection (now at Wollaton Hall, Nottingham); John Fraser Collection (now at Wolverhampton Art Gallery and Museum).

Material from a number of these collections is also held at the British Geological Survey at Keyworth including T.W. Fletcher, C. Ketley, J. Gray and S.H. Blackwell.

A number of small collections have been donated to Dudley Museum in recent years, including A.J. Morris (1988), W. Foxall (1991), D. Ray (1990), A. Barnett (1990) and G. Worton (1992). In 1987 Dudley Museum received the collection bought in an antique shop in 1979 by Mrs Joyce Wedge of Southampton. Formerly the collection of H.L. Haroun of Reigate, Surrey, this contained over 60 Dudley fossils including a *Temnocrinus* from the collection of John Gray which was exhibited at the original B.A. meeting in Dudley in 1839.

Major strengths:

Comprehensive range of invertebrate fauna from the Silurian (Wenlock and Ludlow) rocks of the Dudley/Walsall area, particularly the Much Wenlock Limestone Formation. Also flora and fauna from the local Coal Measures, notably ironstone nodules from Coseley.

Number of specimens:

c.10,000; 5 types, 15 figured, 2 referred.

Displays:

Many of the finest specimens in the collection are on display in the Museum's small Geological Gallery. Originally opened in 1965 the gallery has been refurbished and reopened in November 1992 as *The Time Trail*. Its primary theme is the changing environments in the Black Country throughout geological time. These are depicted by a series of detailed dioramas juxtaposed with fossil rich rock faces, so that the link between past and present is illustrated in a simple yet strikingly visual way. Special displays include a Black Country mining diorama showing both over and underground workings, an exhibit on fluorescent fossils and the "Thumb's-Up" scheme.

Research facilities:

Study area in geology store with binocular microscope. Technician's room with pneumatic development equipment and range of conservation/preparation chemicals. Small library with comprehensive range of literature on local material.

Current projects:

Further refurbishment of the Geological Gallery including installation of interactive computer workstation and audio facilities. Concept planning for a new earth science teaching centre to open late 1994. Concept planning for new interpretation facilities at Castle Hill, Dudley and Wren's Nest National Nature Reserve. These centres would be prime Earth Science attractions and greatly extend the existing geological service. The geological collection would probably be re-housed and displayed at one of these new sites.

Computer cataloguing of the collection began in 1992 and should be complete by March 1994. The museum acts as the Geological Locality Records Centre for the Black Country and is networked into Dudley's Geographical Information System (GIS), which includes digitised records of all the borough's SSSI's and RIG's.

Staff:

Curator, C.G.R. Reid, BA.

Other information:

Other geological resources in close proximity include the Lapworth Museum at Birmingham University (10 miles) and Birmingham Art Gallery and Museum (12 miles).

Compiler:

C.G.R. Reid.

MIDLANDS

HEREFORD

Hereford City Museum

Address:
Broad Street, Hereford, HR4 9AU. Telephone 0432 268121, Ext 207 or 334.

Administration:
Hereford City Council.

Admission:
Free.

Times of opening:
Closed Sunday, Monday.

History:

Main collections built up by members of the Woolhope Naturalist's Field Club during Victorian and Edwardian times.

Major strengths:

Local material.

Number of specimens:

c. 10,000; no types, some figured.

Published catalogues:

Catalogue of fossil fish available.

Displays:

Small display in Museum.

Compiler:

J. Cooter.

MIDLANDS
LEICESTER
Leicestershire Museums, Arts and Records Service

Address:
The Rowans, College Street, Leicester, LE2 0JJ.
Telephone 0533 473080; Fax 0533 473011.

Administration:
Leicestershire County Council.

Admission:
Free.

Times of opening:
Monday - Saturday 10.00 - 17.30, Sunday 14.00 - 17.30.

History:
The collections were founded in 1839 as part of the Leicester Literary and Philosophical Society Museum, although the first recorded geology acquisition dates from 1841. The Leicester Town Museum took over the collections in 1849; subsequently the museum became Leicester Museum and Art Gallery (1881), City of Leicester Museum and Art Gallery (1919) and Leicestershire Museum, Art Galleries and Records Service (1974). The Geology Section, which had its first curator in 1872, became the Earth Sciences section in 1974.

Principal collections:
George Abbot, Beeby Thompson (part), F.W. Bennett, T.O. Bosworth, Montagu Browne, A.R. Bunting, R.F. Damon sale (part), Grantham Museum (part), A.R. Horwood, R.J. King (part), Leicester Literary and Philosophical Society, Loughborough Museum (part), E.E. Lowe, D.M. Martill, S.R. Pattison, Peterborough Museum (part), R. Darell Smyth Stephens (includes S.S. Buckman material), R. Swales, C. Trelease, B.N. Wale, H. Willoughby-Ellis.

Major strengths:
Charnian (Precambrian) holotypes (partly on loan from Leicester University), lithological collections from original mapping of Charnwood Forest, world-wide minerals including Leicestershire specialities, Upper Carboniferous plants from Leicestershire and South Derbyshire coalfield, Liassic and Callovian marine vertebrates from Barrow-upon-Soar

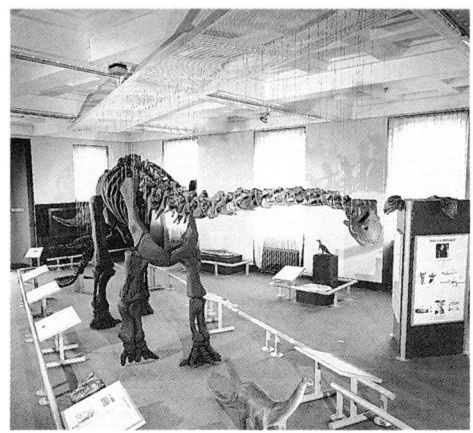

Cetiosaurus – "The Rutland Dinosaur"

(some with soft tissue preservation) and Peterborough, the middle Jurassic sauropod dinosaur, *Cetiosaurus*, from Rutland.

Number of specimens:
c. 58,000.

Published catalogues:
Sizer, C.J. 1960. *Catalogue of type, figured and cited specimens.* Leicestershire Museums Service.

Displays:
The shapes, colours and uses of minerals; past landscapes of Leicestershire; the rocks, fossils and minerals of the county, including *Charnia* and other Precambrian fossils; the Barwell meteorite; Jurassic marine reptiles and the dinosaurs *Cetiosaurus*, *Megalosaurus* and *Plateosaurus*.

Programme of temporary exhibits.

Staff:
Keeper of Earth Sciences, John Martin, BSc, DipMA; Assistant Keeper (Palaeontology), post vacant; Assistant Keeper (Geology and Sites), Gill Weightman, BA; Assistant Keeper (Conservation), Grace Griffith; Assistant Keeper (Interpretation), post vacant.

Compiler:
J.G. Martin.

MIDLANDS
LUDLOW
Ludlow Museum

Address:
Castle Street, Ludlow, SY8 1AS. Telephone 0584 875384. Address for correspondence: Old Street, Ludlow, SY8 1NW. Telephone 0584 873857.

Administration:
Shropshire County Council.

Admission:
Adults 50p; children, UB40 holders, senior citizens free. To Old Street offices and reference collections, by appointment only.

Times of opening:
April - September: Monday -Saturday 10.30 -13.00, 14.00 - 17.00; June - August: Sundays also at these hours.

History:

Established in 1833 with the founding of the Ludlow Natural History Society. The first collections acquired included geological specimens from William Jones, "a keen fossil collector" and the first Hon. Curator. Amongst the instigators of the Society were a group of remarkable amateur geologists including the Rev. T.T. Lewis and Dr Thomas Lloyd who shared their knowledge of the locality with Sir Roderick Impey Murchison when he began his work on the Silurian System. During the 19th century both the Society and its museum thrived, enjoying a high geological reputation.

Following the First World War interest declined. In 1940 the remaining members of the Natural History Society gave the museum collections to Shropshire County Council. The Society was wound up in 1941. In 1946 the first specimens were transferred to the British Museum (Natural History). A new museum at the Butter Cross was opened in 1955, but geology was not featured prominently and much of the original collection was dispersed.

The history of the present collections dates from the appointment of John Norton as curator in 1959. As a result of his hard work, dedication and enthusiasm over the last 30 years, a large and valuable scientific collection has been assembled which, like the original collection, has gained a national, if not international, reputation.

Principal collections:

Comprehensive collections of Palaeozoic fossils from south Shropshire, north Herefordshire and the Welsh borderlands (especially Silurian material). Particularly important are collections of brachiopods, bivalves, trilobites and cephalopods, and notable collections of early fossil fish. Collectors include R. Smith, H.H. Shephard, D. Shutt, J. Dalingwater, W.J. Norton, D. Antia, F.B. Kelly, J. Zalasiewiaz, J.E. Jackson, M. Rowlands, P. Tarrant and Shropshire Geological Society.

Other collections of interest include the Bakes & Coalvin Collection of mammal and reptile bones from the Silwalik Hills (donated in 1840).

Archives:

Archival material relating to Ludlow National History Society and its museum; including a large wall-mounted section through the Welsh Borders made by Murchison to illustrate a lecture he gave in Ludlow in the 1850s.

Major strengths:

Palaeozoic fossils from south Shropshire and the Welsh Borders; high standards of documentation maintained throughout, including good locality detail, mostly from extant sites.

Number of specimens:

35,000-40,000 fossils, 1,500 minerals, 1,000 rocks.

Publications:

Of several guides to the local geology by W.J. Norton, and published by the Shropshire County Museum Service, only *Old Red Sandstone fishes of South Shropshire* is still in print.

Also: Norton, W.J. 1978. Silurian cephalopods of the Welsh Borderland. *Caradoc and Severn valley Field Club Occasional Paper*, **1**.

Lloyd, D. 1983. *The history of Ludlow Museum 1833-1983*. Shrophire Museums Service.

Displays:

Reading the Rocks, an exhibition celebrating Ludlow's contribution to international geology (open July 1994).

Public services:

Handling sessions for schools. (For further details contact the Education Officer, Jayne Speakman, telephone 0743 254008.) Access to reference collections by individuals and groups by appointment only (in writing please, to the Curator of Natural Sciences).

Staff:

Curator of Natural Sciences, Jane E. Mee, PhD.

Other information:

Sales point, including geological publications pertinent to the area. The museum acts as the Geological Locality Records Centre for Shropshire and collaborates with Shropshire Geological Society on the designation of RIGS. The museum is within walking distance of several important geological outcrops such as Ludford Corner, Whitcliffe and Mortimer Forest.

Compiler:

J.E. Mee.

MIDLANDS
NOTTINGHAM
British Geological Survey

Address:
Headquarters: Keyworth, Nottingham, NG12 5GG. Telephone 0602 363100 (Central Enquiries 0602 363143; Fax 0602 363276.)

Access point for BGS publications, information and sales: Geological Museum, Exhibition Road, South Kensington, London, SW7 2DE. Telephone 071 589 4090/938 9056/ 938 9057; Fax 071 584 8270.

Edinburgh Office: Murchison House, West Mains Road, Edinburgh, EH9 3LA. Telephone 031 667 1000; Fax 031 668 2683.

Administration:
BGS is a constituent part of the Natural Environment Research Council.

Admission:
The only public access is to the BGS libraries at Keyworth and Edinburgh, which is free of charge. There are no displays open to the public on BGS premises.

Times of opening (Library):
Monday - Thursday 09.00 - 17.00, Friday 09.00 - 16.30. Closed Bank Holidays.

History:

The Geological Survey was effectively founded in 1835 although geological staff were employed by the "Board of Ordnance" from 1814, later forming the Geological Survey Branch of the Ordnance Survey. Between 1851 and 1935 the Survey was administered from the Museum of Practical Geology in Jermyn Street, London. The Survey then moved, for 50 years, to the purpose-built Geological Museum in Exhibition Road. During and since this time the Survey has functioned under various Government Departments and for a period (1965-1983) carried the less familiar title of "Institute of Geological Sciences" following its amalgamation with the Overseas (previously Colonial) Geological Surveys.

Principal collections:

The Survey has very large holdings of rock specimens, drill core, cuttings and other samples derived mainly from sites in the UK and its continental shelf. These are linked to data on UK geology collected over the last 150 years. It also has substantial map collections and data

Borehole core storage, National Geoscience Data Centre, Keyworth

holdings on the geology of many other countries, especially those in which BGS staff have worked or are working. At present BGS holds only small numbers of overseas specimens, but these are increasing as collections are made to assist overseas work funded by the Overseas Development Administration, the EC and other multilateral funding agencies and by governments.

Biostratigraphic Collections: Palaeontological collecting in the last century provided part of the underlying framework for the first systematic geological survey of the UK. The remapping programme is backed up by further detailed collecting from many sequences and boreholes, some of which were drilled for BGS to resolve stratigraphical problems. The collections contain many specimens from classical localities and some associated with well known geological personalities. New material is also acquired as donations from research workers. Part of the collection is ordered by geological age and taxonomy. This "Type and Stratigraphic Collection" contains over 250,000 specimens illustrative of the taxonomic diversity of the Survey collection. The largest donation, of about 35,000 specimens, was the UK specimens from the Geological Society of London's collection. Donated in 1912, this is also indexed by donor. The Biostratigraphy Group holds indexed records of donations and purchases dating back to 1850. Collections from Northern Ireland are held on behalf of the Department of Commerce of Northern Ireland.

Drill Core and Cuttings Collections: These contain material from over 13,000 boreholes. In the last ten years extensive use has been made of facilities to slice selected intervals of core and retain these as well as sets of specimens and samples. By volume the lengths of core, sliced core and samples probably represent between 1/2 and 2/3rds of the total material in the BGS. There are a further 0.9 million specimens from these and other boreholes; these include many donated to BGS by other organisations. BGS has a statutory right to material and information from certain types of borehole; some of these may be retained "in confidence" for various periods of time. This collection of rock is backed up by a very large collection of data, both published and unpublished, about these and many other boreholes put down for mineral exploration, water, site investigation and other purposes. Many have been geologically classified during the production of more recent maps, memoirs or for other projects. Borehole records are primarily registered geographically by their kilometre grid square and record number.

Offshore Geological Collections and Geochemical databases: Material from over 30,000 sea-bed sample stations and over 500 boreholes may be consulted via BGS Central Enquiries. Original core and sample material is available for inspection. Particle size analysis and offshore geochemical data can be abstracted via the BGS Oracle database as either raw data or map formats. Seismic track data and bathymetric data are also held. BGS offshore core and sample material may be at either Keyworth or Edinburgh.

Mineralogy and Petrology Collections: Rocks, thin sections, minerals and chemically analysed rock powders represent specimens systematically collected by Survey staff for the 1-inch and 1:50K geological mapping programme. Between 1984 and 1987, various collections from the former Leeds, Exhibition Road and Gray's Inn Road, London, offices were moved to Keyworth. Collections which relate to Scottish geology are curated in Murchison House, Edinburgh. Systematic databasing of paper records relating to these collections was begun in 1985 and currently some 105,000 records have been transferred to the PetMin Databank.

Archives:

The BGS Library: Collections date back well over 150 years and include an international range of geological literature and archives. It holds over 500,000 volumes, 200,000 maps, 14,000 serial titles, 75,000 photographs of geological interest, including the "British Association" collection of geological photographs, and over 30,000 archive items. Manual and some digital indexes provide ready access. Progress is being made to digitize many of the in-house indexes. These will then complement a range of commercial bibliographic databases accessed via DIALOG etc. or held in the form of CD-ROM services, e.g. Georef and Geoarchive. The Library and Records are places of deposit under the Public Records Act. The Library is open to the public for consultation, but not for the borrowing of material.

The National Geological Records Centres at Keyworth and Edinburgh: These hold the records from over 500,000 boreholes and over 15,000 site investigation reports for the UK. They also contain collections of over 50,000 original UK manuscript geological maps and geologists' field slips, as well as large quantities of unpublished data in the form of plans, archived field notebooks, etc.

UK Land Survey: Through the six offices in Britain and Northern Ireland, the Survey undertakes multidisciplinary mapping and issues resurveyed, partial revision and provisional maps, mainly at 1:10K and 1:50K scales. It plans to have a complete 1:50K series, covering the UK landmass, available within about 15 years. The revision programme is to be backed up by a digital map production system also producing special scale thematic maps for land-use planning, e.g. sand and gravel, geological hazards etc. This is coupled with extensive data gathering of both digital and analogue data. Current documents such as field records, maps, aerial photographs, mine plans, records on boreholes and temporary sections are also held, many of which can be consulted.

Geophysical Survey data for UK and overseas: The digital database for the National Gravity Survey of the UK includes gravity data, validated and adjusted to international standards, from over 150,000 stations on land and over 270,000 line km of shipborne gravity data for the continental shelf. A similar dataset records the National Magnetic Survey covering the land area, and part of the continental shelf, with airborne traverse data at 2km intervals, and the remainder of the shelf with shipborne traverses. This information has mainly been generated by manually digitising original analogue survey data. Analogue records, with a digital index, are held of geophysical logs of 5,000 boreholes on the UK landmass.

Geochemical database: This holds chemical data and supporting information derived from over 0.5 million samples of rock, soil, stream sediments and water, analysed for many elements by a variety of methods. The results are held on an Oracle database. Publications include Geochemical Atlases and more than 100 Mineral Reconnaissance Reports. The latter includes accounts of the discoveries of precious metal mineralisation in Scotland and SW England and of the major baryte deposit near Aberfeldy.

Global Seismology; Geomagnetism: Systematic monitoring is carried out from over 100 seismographs in the UK. The detailed investigation of British earthquakes is backed up by a substantial archive on historic earthquakes, also by a database on seismic events related to mining subsidence. This constitutes a national seismic information service, based in Edinburgh. Automatic recording and data processing from 3 UK geomagnetic observatories allows daily (or even hourly) access by users. The UK magnetic survey complements this and allows precise modelling of the main geomagnetic field and its secular changes in and around the UK. Information is currently exchanged daily with 15 international observatories and this network is being extended. Disturbance data and forecasts of disturbance levels are made for both science and commerce, e.g. to help in precise navigation and to predict induced currents in pipe or power lines.

Hydrogeological and Geotechnical Databases: These hold records of about 120,000 water wells, water level variations with time in over 150 of these wells, hydrogeochemical analyses on about 25,000 water samples, aquifer physical properties such as permeability and porosity for over 20,000 rock samples and geotechnical properties for about 100,000 rock and soil samples. Data may be in analogue or digital form. Many of the analogue data are currently being digitised, at least to index level. The databases support hydrogeological, hydrogeochemical and engineering geology surveys concerned with the exploration, development, management and protection of groundwater resources; with the safe disposal of hazardous wastes on land, and with the assessment of geological conditions for civil engineering purposes.

Number of specimens:

The biostratigraphical collections contain over 1.5 million specimens and over 150,000 slides of microfossils. Approximately 30,000 are type, figured or referred specimens and there are also over 10,000 similarly referred microfossils. Plus approximately 252,000 rocks, thin sections, minerals and (wet) chemically analysed rock powders.

Displays:

Displays on site illustrate recent BGS research or demonstrate the many practical applications of the science of geology and can be seen on educational visits by arrangement. There are no displays available to the casual visitor.

Public services:

Reception areas at the Keyworth Headquarters and at the London and Edinburgh offices have sales desks through which Geological Survey maps and publications can be ordered; a small range of other products (wall charts, fossil replicas, rock specimens) are also sold. Public lectures, meetings and "Open Days" are locally advertised. Tours of the Keyworth site may be arranged by applying to the Survey's Corporate Coordination and Information Division. Visitors requiring to consult BGS staff are requested to make an appointment. No fees are currently charged for advice on the availability of information or of a service. However, a schedule of fees may apply where access to the collection or the provision of information requires time to be spent by BGS staff. Nevertheless, fees may be waived where an enquiry, including the loan of specimens, is certified as being for bona-fide research.

Research facilities:

BGS is equipped with a wide variety of modern scientific facilities which are primarily assigned to current BGS projects. The "Type and Stratigraphic Collection" is available to research workers by arrangement. Fees may be charged for use of facilities or of staff time.

Current projects:

Development of relational geological databases to integrate BGS data on specimens by location, geological age, lithology, mineralogy, bios tratigraphy, geophysics, geochemistry and other fields. Development of methods to hold and retrieve data in digital form about BGS maps.

Compiler:

H.C. Ivimey-Cook (and published with the approval of the Director, British Geological Survey (NERC)).

MIDLANDS

NOTTINGHAM
Nottingham Natural History Museum

Address:
Wollaton Hall, Nottingham, NG8 2AE. Telephone 0602 281333/281130.

Administration:
Nottingham City Council.

Admission:
Monday - Friday free, Saturdays, Sundays and Bank Holidays adults £1.00; children 50p; Museums Association members free.

Times of opening:
April - September: Monday - Saturday 10.00 -19.00, Sunday 14.00 - 17.00; October - March: 10.00 - 16.30, Sunday 13.30 - 16.30. Closed December 25th.

History:

The first public natural history museum in Nottingham was established in 1867 and consisted of "a collection of natural history, botanical, geological and other specimens, mineralogy, antiquities and general curiosities made by the Nottingham Naturalists Society (now defunct), the Committee of the Mechanics Institution and the trustees of the late Mr George Walker" (Jones, 1937). The Museum first opened to the public on the 16th April, 1872. With the growth in size and importance of the collections came the need for bigger and better accommodation so, in 1881, the museum was moved to a specially built west wing of the University College building in central Nottingham.

In 1925 Wollaton Hall and the surrounding park was bought by Nottingham Corporation from Lord Middleton and a year later the museum's collections were transferred here from the University College. In 1927 the entire administration of the Natural History Museum passed from the University to the Nottingham Corporation and Professor J.W. Carr was appointed Curator.

Principal collections:

Since the establishment of the Museum in 1867, the geological collections have been added to continuously with some large and many small donations and purchases. Important rock and mineral collections include minerals from the west coast of S. America donated by Mr G.T. Davy around 1860, Spanish ores and rocks donated by Mr F. Gillman (1845-1926) and minerals, mainly Cornish, donated by Mr H. Crowther (1848-1937).

The fossils collections have been built up over the years by museum staff and by important donations and consist of a wide range of British fossils from throughout the Phanerozoic. Important collections include Pleistocene mammals from Creswell Crags from the Rev. J. Magens Mello (1836-1914), British fossils from the Rev. T.C.B. Chamberlin (19th century), Upper Carboniferous plants from Derbyshire and Nottinghamshire from Mr A.R. Horwood (1879-1937), Silurian fossils from Dudley from Mr E.J. Hollier (19th century), Crag vertebrates from Mr E. Charlesworth (1813-1893), Carboniferous Limestone fossils from Mr Samuel Carrington (1798-1870), Permo-Triassic footprints from Professor H.H. Swinnerton (1875-1966) and others.

Number of specimens:

c. 40,000 fossils, c. 4,000 minerals, c. 1,000 rocks; 42 type, figured, or referred fossils.

Published catalogues:

Turner, N.S. 1990. The mineral collection of the Natural History Museum, Wollaton Hall, Nottingham. *U.K. Journal of Mines and Minerals,* **8**, 15-17.

Jones, H.P. 1937. Some notable museums XX - The Nottingham Natural History Museum. *The North Western Naturalist,* 1-10.

Displays:
Mineral Gallery with systematic arrangement of minerals based on chemical composition, plus display of exceptional specimens. Fossil Gallery displays *The Fossil Story* which recreates seven landscapes from the Phanerozoic.

Staff:
Keeper of Geology, Neil S. Turner.

Other information:
The museum acts as the Geological Locality Records Centre for Nottinghamshire and has recently produced the first Geological Site Alert Schedule for the county.

Compiler:
N.S. Turner.

MIDLANDS
SHREWSBURY
Rowley's House

Address:
Barker Street, Shrewsbury, SY1 1QH. Telephone 0743 361196.

Administration:
Shrewsbury Museum Service, Shrewsbury and Atcham Borough Council.

Admission:
Adults £1.20; senior citizens, students £0.80; children £0.50.

Times of opening:
Monday - Saturday 10.00 - 17.00, Sunday (summer only) 11.00 - 16.00.

History:

Founded 1938. The origin of the geology collection dates back to the establishment of the Shropshire and North Wales Natural History Society in 1835. Later, in 1877, the Society was amalgamated to form the Shropshire Archaeological and Natural History Society. The new Society's collections were displayed in the museum on College Hill, Shrewsbury.

In 1884 the collections were moved to the Old Grammar School Buildings, Castlegate, property of the Shrewsbury Corporation. It was opened a year later as a new Free Museum and Library, the geological collection having been arranged by Dr Charles Callaway, the pioneer of Pre-Cambrian research. During its history the collection has been fortunate in having a succession of good geologists, either as curators or advisors who not only applied their scholarship, but also enhanced it from their own collections. The ownership of the collections was transferred to Shrewsbury Corporation in 1895 and that year Calloway was appointed the first Hon. Curator. Valuable assistance was also given by another distinguished Cambrian geologist, Edgar Sterling Cobbold.

Dr Calloway was succeeded by a local geologist, R.A. Buddicom and later by Rev. W.M.D. de la Touche, the son of one of Britain's best known nineteenth century amateur geologists, the Rev. James Digues de la Touche. In 1928 the Museum sought the help of Dr W.F. Whittard (later Professor of Geology, Bristol University) with the identification and rearrangement of the collection. In 1936 Whittard accepted the appointment as Hon. Curator and the Museum was successful in its application to the Carnegie United Kingdom Trust for a grant towards the re-organisation of the geology collection. The new displays were completed in 1938.

At the end of the 1940's the collections were transferred to Rowley's House and again another local geologist, J.T. Wattison, acting as Hon. Adviser, undertook the task of reorganisation. In 1952 a collection of Coalbrookdale Coal Measures specimens were transferred from the Walker Technical College, Oakengates, to the Museum. During his supervision of the move, Wattison recognised important scientific material belonging to the missing Reynolds-Anstice Collection. This along with other type and figured material was passed to the BM(NH) in 1956.

In the late 1970's the collection was moved into a basement room before extension work began on Rowley's House. A new geology gallery was opened to the public in November 1982.

Principal collections:

A major part of the geological collection consists of Shropshire fossils and rocks. Most specimens are reasonably documented. Besides providing a good reference to Shropshire's varied geology, the collection has important historic value. Many specimens come from the collections of noted Shropshire geologists and researchers including Charles Callaway, Edgar Sterling Cobbold, Rev. W.M.D. de la Touche, George Cocking, Charles Fortey, C.J. Stubberfield, J.F. Walker, W.W. Watts, W.F. Whittard, J.T. Wattison, R.A. Buddicom and A. M. Davies. The discovery that the Walker Technical College Collection was in fact the remains of the lost Reynolds-Anstice Collection adds further historic interest.

These named collections are incorporated into the general stratigraphic collection together with the considerable collection of Canon William Kitely Wylie.

The specimens of the Walker Technical College Collection consists mainly of plant and fish fragments from the Middle Coal Measures of Coalbrookdale, but also include some Triassic reptile remains and footprints (mainly *Rhynchosaurus* from Grinshill). The collection also includes Jurassic fossils donated by H. Iken from Prees Heath.

The mineral collection is world-wide, but includes Shropshire minerals from Shelve and Snailbeach. Most of these are from the collections of Captain Oldfield, J.T. Wattison and R. and J. Pugh. The small rock collection includes samples of Shropshire building stones and roadstones.

Archives:

Donation books of the Shropshire and North Wales Natural History Society, Library and Museum Committee Minutes, accession books (1977), papers and correspondence relating to the collection and collectors, plus a reference library containing nineteenth century books and periodicals.

Major strengths:

A comprehensive collection of Shropshire rocks, fossils and minerals from a wide range of sites. Cambrian and Ordovician strata are well represented and there is a good selection of Silurian fossils. Specimens from the Coal Measures include some good quality plants. The Triassic reptile specimens have been cited by A.S. Woodward and C. Beasley.

Number of specimens:

3,200 fossils, 200 rocks, 500 minerals.

Displays:

The small gallery on the first floor of Rowley's House is mainly devoted to the geology of Shropshire. Its main theme is the county's geological history, but other aspects include an introduction to geology, Shropshire's geologists, minerals, building stones and roadstones. The Triassic reptiles from Grinshill are displayed along with a model of a rhynchosaur.

Compiler:

Rosemary Roden.

MIDLANDS
STOKE-ON-TRENT
Stoke-on-Trent City Museum and Art Gallery

Address:
Bethesda Street, Hanley, Stoke-on-Trent, ST1 3DE.
Telephone 0782 202173; Fax 0782 205033.

Administration:
Stoke-on-Trent City Council.

Admission:
Free.

Times of opening:
Monday - Saturday 10.00 - 17.00, Sunday 14.00 - 17.00.

History:

The geological material is now housed in a purpose-built museum opened in 1981, but the formation of collections stems from the activities of the North Staffordshire Field Club during several decades after their formation in 1865. The NSFC succeeded in opening a Natural History Museum as part of the existing Hanley Museum in 1908 and concentrated on displaying and collecting material specific to the local area. The Club included within its membership such notables as John Ward, Robert Garner and Wheelton Hind along with many other enthusiasts. During the middle years of the 20th century interest in the Museum decreased and it was not until the upgrading of facilities in the late 1970's that the Natural History Section was able to specifically appoint a member of staff with geological training. In 1978 a rationalisation of Natural History specimens in Staffordshire led to the transfer of all the geological material from Shugborough Museum to Stoke.

Principal collections:

Two collections are retained as individual entities: John Ward Collection of Carboniferous fish fossils (c. 800 specimens), representing the majority of the Coal Measure fish species to be found in the North Staffordshire Coalfield; W.A.S. Sarjeant Collection of North Midlands minerals (c. 1,000 specimens), mainly from Derbyshire and Shropshire, collected between 1953 and 1970.

Natural History Gallery

Major strengths:

The collection as a whole is particularly strong in locally collected specimens belonging to the Carboniferous and Triassic; approximately 80% of the total fossil material is from the North Staffordshire Carboniferous. There is a representative collection of minerals and good collections of both Upper Carboniferous fossils and local Carboniferous and Triassic rocks.

Number of specimens:

c. 5,000 fossils, c. 2,500 minerals, c. 2,500 rocks; no holotypes, 100 other status specimens.

Published catalogues:

Catalogues of the Sarjeant mineral collection and Ward fish fossils are available.

Displays:

Geology forms part of the integrated Natural History Gallery which depicts how the various habitats of Staffordshire relate to their underlying strata. Temporary exhibitions are used to show more general geology aspects not covered in the permanent gallery.

Staff:

Senior Assistant Keeper of Natural History (Geology), D.I. Steward.

Other information:

The museum acts as the Geological Locality Records Centre for Staffordshire.

Compiler:

D.I. Steward.

MIDLANDS
TELFORD
Jackfield Tile Museum

Address:
Jackfield, Ironbridge, Telford, TF8 7AW. Telephone 0952 882030.

Administration:
The Ironbridge Gorge Museum Trust.

Admission:
Adults £3.00; senior citizens £2.45; students, children (over 5) £1.80.

Times of opening:
Every day 10.00 - 17.00.

History:

In 1985 the Ironbridge Gorge Museum Trust launched a new scheme to introduce geological and mining material into its collections and displays. The Museum's goal in this was to emphasise the relationship between economic geology and industrial development.

The first step was to form a Mining and Geology Group made up of members of the museum's staff, academic and professional geologists, mining experts and industrialists. This group provided valuable assistance in the first major acquisition under the scheme, the George Maw Collection, Maw being head of the large nineteenth century decorative tile company based in the Ironbridge Gorge at Jackfield.

It was natural, therefore, to site the Museum's economic geology gallery, *The Great Rock Sandwich*, at the Trust's Jackfield Tile Museum site.

Principal collections:

George Maw (1832-1912) - chiefly collected in the 1860s, it was originally presented to the Geological Survey's Jermyn Street Museum, and transferred to Ironbridge in 1985; Rowlands and Tarrant Collection - fossils from the Coalbrookdale Shales (Wenlockian), including trilobites, brachiopods, graptolites, bivalves and gastropods.

Number of specimens:
c.5,000.

Displays:

The Great Rock Sandwich - a new gallery which focuses on the Coalbrookdale Coalfield as an example of the link between geology and industrial development. Visitors enter the gallery through a section of Coal Measures and pass images of the industries which exploited them. They are able to touch the raw materials of coal, limestone, ironstone and clay before entering an adit, where they discover how miners and geologists learnt about the coalfield. The final section covers the demise of deep mining on the coalfield and the rise of opencast and its economics.

Current projects:

Production of a teacher's pack to complement the new gallery; development of schools' loan collection; input of collection documentation onto Museum's MODES system.

Staff:
Curator, Michael Vanns.

Compiler:
K. Foster.

MIDLANDS
WARWICK
Warwickshire Museum

Address:
Market Place, Warwick, CV34 4SA. Telephone 0926 412500/412481.

Administration:
Warwickshire County Council.

Admission:
Free.

Times of opening:
Monday - Saturday 10.00 - 17.30, Sunday (May - September only) 14.30 - 17.00.

History:
Originally the collections were built up by Warwickshire Natural History and Archaeological Society which was formed in 1836. A Society museum opened the following year, open to members only, but also to the public on special occasions at a charge of one shilling. The Warwickshire Naturalist and Archaeologist Field Club, established in 1855, resulted in a major increase in the number of acquisitions. However, the Society went into a gradual decline at the end of the nineteenth century and by 1891 there were only 31 members. In 1932 the Society offered the entire collection to the County Council who, in accepting the offer, became the first county authority in Britain to take over responsibility for a museum service. In 1938 a professional curator was appointed and the museum re-opened to the public in 1951. In 1960 a Deputy Curator and Keeper of Geology was appointed. The Geology Gallery was completely re-displayed in 1974.

Principal collections:
Rev. P.B. Brodie; John William Kirshaw; Dr George Lloyd; Knecht Collection of minerals; William Creighton Maclean; Leamington Museum and Art Gallery.

Major strengths:
Triassic vertebrate fossils, including several type and figured specimens; Lower Jurassic fossils in general.

Number of specimens:
c. 15,000; c.100 status specimens.

Reconstruction of Dasyceps bucklandi, *from the Permian of Kennilworth*

Displays:
One ground floor gallery designed by Colin Milne in 1974. Displays feature introduction to geology; series of stratigraphic cases dealing with Warwickshire geology; two mineral cases; three panels on formation of rocks; two cases on Rev. P.B. Brodie; one skeleton of Irish Giant Deer; one skeleton of Plesiosaur; one audio-visual display showing man's use of Warwickshire's rocks entitled *No Stone Unturned*.

Staff:
Keeper of Geology, John Crossling, BSc, AMA.

Other information:
The museum acts as the Geological Locality Records Centre for Warwickshire which has some 1,500 locations both current and historic on file.

Compiler:
J. Crossling.

MIDLANDS

WOLVERHAMPTON
Wolverhampton Art Gallery and Museum

Address:
Lichfield Street, Wolverhampton, WV1 1DU.
Telephone 0902 312032.

Administration:
Wolverhampton Metropolitan Borough Council.

Admission:
Free.

Times of opening:
Monday - Saturday 10.00 - 17.00.

History:

Founded in 1884. In 1911 the geological collection of Dr John Fraser (1820-1909), a local medical practitioner, was bequeathed to the Borough of Wolverhampton on the condition that the specimens were displayed in a public building. The collection of 10,000 specimens was moved to the Art Gallery in 1914 and displayed in the North Room until 1938. During the Second World War the collection was stored in the Central Library and then transferred in 1952 to Wolverhampton Technical College. In 1970, when the Technical College became a Polytechnic, the best specimens were abstracted for a teaching collection and the remainder were removed to Himley Hall. In the early 1980's the deteriorating state of the collection and the disappearance of specimens, including the entire mineral collection, became a subject of concern and a campaign was started to try and save this once fine collection. In 1984 the collection was returned to Wolverhampton Art Gallery and Museum and a rescue curation commenced. The new museum extension, completed in 1987, includes a small gallery for the display of the Fraser Collection.

Principal collections:

The major collection, the Fraser Collection, assembled in the last part of the nineteenth century, is comprised almost totally of fossils. It includes several specimens collected by noted Midland geologists (Professor C. Lapworth, Rev. P. Brodie, Rev. W. Symonds and Mr John Ward). With the exception of a collection of

Lepidotus from the Lower Lias

Caenozoic molluscs from the Paris Basin, the material comes from British and local sites. The specimens have a wide stratigraphic range, from Cambrian to Pleistocene, with particular emphasis on the Silurian and Jurassic. Most groups of invertebrates are represented, especially brachiopods and ammonites. The collection also contains a good selection of plant fossils from the Coal Measures. The Fraser Collection includes some high quality specimens and was originally well documented. Others include the Mrs Tildesley Bequest of rocks and minerals, and the Bilston Library Collection of local fossils, transferred in 1987.

Major strengths:

Local Silurian fossils, Coal Measures plants, Jurassic ammonites and Caenozoic molluscs. Figured graptolites from the Fraser Collection are now in the Lapworth Museum, University of Birmingham.

Number of specimens:

7,000 fossils, 200 minerals, 200 rocks.

Displays:

Fossil display, particularly aimed at younger ages, opening 1994.

Public services:

Activities for school parties in preparation. Education room within the Museum. Identification and other enquiries dealt with on request.

Compiler:

Rosemary Roden.

MIDLANDS
WORCESTER
Worcester City Museum and Art Gallery

Address:
Foregate Street, Worcester, WR1 1DT. Telephone 0905 723471; Fax 0905 20781.

Administration:
Worcester City Council.

Admission:
Free.

Times of opening:
Monday, Tuesday, Wednesday, Friday 09.30 - 18.00, Saturday 09.30 - 17.00.

History:

On April 8th 1833 Dr Charles Hastings presided at the inaugural meeting of the Worcestershire Natural History Society at the Guildhall, Worcester. The object of the Society was that "the knowledge of natural history may be more widely spread, local observations concentrated, and remarkable specimens illustrative of the several branches of science observed". By July 1833 the Curator, George Reece, was able to begin a collection of various specimens concerning natural history and geology.

The first museum of the Society was in the recently vacated old City Library premises in Angel Street. Non-members were allowed in on Mondays, Wednesdays and Saturdays between 11.00am and 5.00pm for a charge of one shilling. By 1835 the premises were already overcrowded as the collection of specimens grew. Thus a Museum Building Society was formed to raise funds for a new building. This venture was highly successful resulting in the new building being opened with great ceremony on September 15th 1836. At this time the Society could boast 325 subscribers, an income of £400 per annum and 2,000 geological specimens. Distinquished visitors such as Charles Lyell and Roderick Murchison were to patronise the museum.

In 1866 Charles Hastings died, his place as President of the Society being taken by his son, George. The Society began to decline in membership and income and the museum was neglected, being linked with the City Library.

In 1879 the City Corporation adopted the Public Libraries Act and the Museum was sold to the Council for £2,820. The Society's collections, library and paintings were donated to the Corporation on two conditions: first that George Reece was retained as Curator, and secondly that the name of the new institution be the "Worcester Public Library and Hastings Museum". These conditions were fulfilled and the institution was opened in 1881.

The Museum and Library moved to its present site in 1896, when a combination of all literary and scientific institutions run by the Corporation were moved to the new site in Foregate Street, known as "The Hastings Museum and Victoria Institute" commemorating the Queen's Diamond Jubilee.

In 1963 the name was changed to the "City Museum"

Principal collections:

Sir Joseph Strutt (minerals); Mr Tennant (minerals); 1861 Malvern Tunnel Collection; Sir Charles Hastings; H.E. Strickland; Rev. W.S. Symonds; Earl of Enniskillen; Rev. Winnington Ingram; Dr Holl.

Major strengths:

Large world-wide mineral collection (3,600 specimens); British fossils, especially from local Silurian and Jurassic; building stones.

Number of specimens:

c. 15,000.

Displays:

Small gallery devoted to Severn Valley geology.

Staff:

No permanent geologist on staff.

Compiler:

I. Rutherford.

EAST-CENTRAL AND SOUTH-EAST ENGLAND

AYLESBURY
Buckinghamshire County Museum

Address:
Church Street, Aylesbury, HP20 2QP. Telephone 0296 88849.

Admission:
Free.

Times of opening:
Monday - Saturday 10.00 - 13.30, 14.00 - 17.00.

History:

The Buckinghamshire Archaeological Society was founded in 1847 and an appeal was made for "the collection of materials sufficient and complete to illustrate the topographical history of the County". After occupying various different premises under a number of Honorary Curators the collections were moved into one part of the buildings it occupies today in 1907. In the new building provision was made for a resident curator's flat and one was duly appointed in 1908. At the same time the title "The Bucks County Museum" was adopted as were daily opening hours. The first annual grant from the County Council was made in 1920, and additional buildings were incorporated into and built onto the Museum in 1934 and 1949. A joint committee of representatives of the Archaeological Society and the County Council was formed in 1951 and a Schools Museum Officer was appointed. In 1957 the Archaeological Society leased the Museum and its contents to the County Council which undertook to maintain the buildings. A further building was purchased in 1960 and a Keeper of Natural History was appointed in 1967.

Principal collections:

F.H. Parrot; T.G. Parrot; F. Codrington; Rev. T. Browne; Dr John Lee; Z.D. Hunt; Newton; J. Rutland; E. Hollis; E. Neaverson; F.A. Lea; K.P Oakley; Bradwell Abbey; M. Oates; W. Rose; W. Goodsir; Pitstone-Marsworth.

Major strengths:

Good quality and extensive stratigraphic collection of Buckinghamshire rocks and fossils with strengths in local Oxfordian, Kimmeridgian,

Portland, Purbeck and Chalk. Vertebrate fossils include Jurassic reptiles (including the recently collected Watermead pliosaur), plus Pleistocene large mammals (including the Pitstone-Marsworth specimens). Also a collection of non-Buckinghamshire rocks and fossils, plus small mineral reference collections.

Number of specimens:

c.12,000 (excluding large collection of Pleistocene bones from Pitstone excavation); at least 8 type specimens plus some figured and referred (including Hartwell Clay and Portlandian ammonites described by S.S. Buckman).

Publications:

Leaflet: *Geology in and around Buckinghamshire.*

Displays:

Limited by current refurbishment, but temporary displays at the Museum and at geological conferences produced.

Current projects:

Museum currently undergoing refurbishment and consequently only two galleries remain open. Occasional geology displays will appear until the complete reopening of the Museum in 1995. An interdisciplinary gallery will include geological exhibits and "visible storage" of specimens. There will also be a children's discovery gallery, where geological material can be made more accessible to visitors. The geology collections and staff are currently located at Buckinghamshire County Museum, Technical Centre, Tring Road, Halton, HP22 5PJ (telephone 0296 696012). There are no galleries in this building, but arrangements to study collections can be made by appointment.

Staff:

Keeper of Biology and Geology, Kate Hawkins; Environmental Records Officer, Julian Scott.

Other information:

The museum acts as the Geological Locality Records Centre for Buckinghamshire and is the centre for the RIGS Group for Buckinghamshire.

Compilers:

J.H. Scott and K.M. Hawkins.

EAST-CENTRAL AND SOUTH-EAST ENGLAND

BRIGHTON
The Booth Museum of Natural History

Address:
194 Dyke Road, Brighton, BN1 5AA. Telephone 0273 552586/713299; Fax 0273 563455.

Administration:
A branch of Brighton Borough Council's Arts & Leisure Department (Royal Pavilion, Art Gallery and Museums section).

Admission:
Free.

Times of opening:
Monday - Wednesday, Friday, Saturday 10.00 - 17.00, Sunday 14.00 - 17.00 (closed Thursday).

History:

Good quality geological specimens were among the very first donations made to Brighton's Town Museum. The Museum was inaugurated by Richard Owen on November 6th 1861. The standard of collections acquired was maintained first under the influence of Henry Willett, a local worthy with a great interest in geology, Thomas Davidson, the brachiopod worker who lived in Brighton, Agnes Crane, his assistant, and her brother, Edward Crane, who succeeded Davidson to the Chairmanship of the Museum sub-committee. In 1888 Thomas Greenwood published his *Museums and Art Galleries* in which he listed Brighton Museum's strengths as "Geology & Archaeology" in the care of Benjamin Lomax, the curator. Lomax produced the first catalogue of the geology collection in 1890.

Despite the fact that a geological curator was never appointed until recent times, the collections continued to be added to throughout the earlier part of the twentieth century. From 1902, the collections were displayed in the newly rebuilt Museum and Art Gallery in Church Street, Brighton where they remained for many years. The geology gallery was closed during the second world war and the collections ultimately packed away and neglected. Indeed, their parlous state aroused some controversy among some eminent workers in the 1960's and 1970's.

Meanwhile, Edward Booth (1840-1890) had opened his "Bird Museum" on the Dyke Road in 1874, a museum which was inherited by the Brighton Corporation on Booth's death. Although the Booth began to acquire some insect collections, it always maintained its individuality from the bird, insect and other collections in the Museum and Art Gallery. This arrangement ended when, from 1975, all Brighton's natural history collections were transferred to the Booth as part of a reorganisation of the town's Royal Pavilion and Museums Department. The geology collections were thus salvaged from threat and they emerged more or less intact from their packing and were sorted, stored and continue even now to be catalogued. The first Keeper of Geology was appointed in 1975.

Principal collections:

George B. Alexander (d.1980) - Carboniferous corals and goniatites; R.M. Brydone (1873-1943) - Chalk echinoids, mostly *Echinocorys*; Agnes Crane (d.1932) - Brachiopods etc.; Arthur F. Griffith (1856-1933) - Cambridge Greensand fossils; Daniel Hack (?d.1913) - minerals; George B. Holmes (1803-1887) - Wealden vertebrates; Charles Potter (1826-1898) - Chalk fossils; Philip J. Rufford (1852-1902) - Wealden plants; Henry Willett (1823-1905) - Chalk fossils, esp. fish etc.; E.A. Jarzembowski (1951-) - Wealden and Carboniferous insects.

Major strengths:

Chalk fossils, especially vertebrates; Lower Cretaceous fossils, especially Wealden; Pleistocene collections, especially caves, Selsey etc.; Wealden and Carboniferous insects.

Number of specimens:

c. 50,000 (90% fossils, 5% minerals, 5% rocks); c. 300 type, figured and referred specimens. A draft catalogue of published specimens has been prepared.

Published catalogues:

Crane, E. 1892. Catalogue of types and figured specimens now in the Brighton Museum. *Report Brighton Public Museum for 1891-1892*, Appendix B, 9-20. [See also *ibid., 1892-1893* which contains note on types added to the collection.]

Willett, H. 1871. *Catalogue of the Cretaceous fossils in the Brighton Museum.*

Other publications:

Anon. 1990. *The Booth Museum of Natural History*. 16pp. Brighton Borough Council. [Handbook celebrating the centenary of the Museum as a public institution.]

Cooper, J.A. 1984. Geological collections and collectors of note: White Watson (1760-1835) in the Booth Museum, Brighton. *Geological Curator* **4**:1, 17-18.

Displays:

There is one permanent gallery devoted to geology in the Museum. It currently houses displays on Chalk and Chalk fossils, flint, Wealden dinosaurs and minerals. In addition, a number of small and large temporary exhibitions on geological themes are mounted from time to time.

Staff:

Keeper of Geology, John A. Cooper, BSc, AMA, FGS.

Other information:

The Booth Museum is a designated Geological Locality Records Centre and holds records relating to over 3,800 sites of geological interest, the majority of which are from published sources. The Museum is the headquarters for the Brighton and Hove Geological Society. The Booth Museum was formerly a part of the Royal Pavilion, Art Gallery and Museums Department, but was amalgamated into an Arts & Leisure Department in 1991.

Compiler:

J.A. Cooper.

EAST-CENTRAL AND SOUTH-EAST ENGLAND

CAMBRIDGE
Sedgwick Museum

Address:
Department of Earth Sciences, Downing Street, Cambridge, CB2 3EQ. Telephone 0223 333456.

Administration:
University of Cambridge.

Admission:
Free.

Times of opening:
In University Full Term: Monday - Friday 09.00 - 13.00, 14.00 - 17.00, Saturday 10.00 - 13.00; additionally by arrangement with the curators. Closed Christmas and Easter.

History:

The museum was effectively founded in 1728 when Dr John Woodward bequeathed his two cabinets of English "fossils" to the University. In 1729 the University purchased, through Woodward's executors, his two remaining cabinets of foreign "fossils" and thus was formed the "Woodwardian Museum". The Woodwardian Professor, whose Chair was also established through Woodward's will, was required to maintain the collections, to demonstrate them and to give public lectures. But it was only when Adam Sedgwick was elected to the Chair in 1818 that teaching began on a regular basis and a Department of Geology grew out of the Museum. The Woodwardian Museum then began rapidly to expand, outgrowing space in the Arts School and later the Divinity School and moving in 1841 into a purpose-built portion of the new Cockrell Building. This too became inadequate and after Sedgwick's death in 1873 his colleagues and the public subscribed towards a new museum as a memorial. This became the present Sedgwick Museum opened in 1904. The museum is now part of the unified Department of Earth Sciences which incorporates the former departments of Geology, Geodesy & Geophysics and Mineralogy & Petrology.

Principal collections:

Apart from John Woodward's original collection (which is Britain's oldest intact geological collection), the museum has several hundred fossil collections, large and small, associated with

named collectors ranging from Mary Anning, William Bean, Thomas Hawkins, Thomas Image and John Leckenby through Sedgwick, Barrande, Darwin, Lyell and Murchison to O.T. Jones, O.M.B. Bulman, C.R.C. Paul, A.T. Thomas and H.B. Whittington. The numerically largest collections are those of R.M. Brydone (c. 40,000 specimens), B.W. Sparks (13,000) and William Walton (11,000). Even though they may be scattered through the museum according to their stratigraphy and provenance, the component specimens of any of these collections can be listed and retrieved, or a full catalogue of them produced through the computer system. There are over 1,600 individual donors in the computer catalogue.

Major strengths:

The collection is a taxonomically and stratigraphically comprehensive reference collection of international scope. One major strength lies in this wide coverage, but perhaps the museum's greatest strength is that the vast bulk of the collection is fully catalogued, the catalogue data rapidly accessible through computer data-handling techniques and all specimens readily accessible to physical examination. The collection is arranged stratigraphically and geographically and within this arrangement taxonomically, so that even the small proportion of uncatalogued material is ordered, sorted and readily examinable.

Number of specimens:

c. 1,000,000 fossils; c. 9,000 types (excluding topotypes), >15,000 figured, >15,000 referred.

Catalogues:

John Woodward's manuscript catalogues and copies of the original printed versions of 1729 are still kept with his collection. Under Sedgwick's direction, important descriptive and taxonomic catalogues of the new collections were prepared by F.W. M'Coy (1851-55), H.G. Seeley (1869, 1870) and J.W. Salter (1873). Henry Woods (1891) published a catalogue of type fossils in the Woodwardian Museum and J. Watson published catalogues of building stones (1911), marbles and ornamental stones (1916) and cements and artificial stones (1922). At the same time the identification and labelling of the rapidly expanding collection involved many individuals - Robert Farren, Walter and Henry Keeping, F.R. Cowper Reed, A.E.N. Arber, W.B.R. King, G.L. Ellis, A.G. Brighton and Dorothy Hill. In 1931 Alfred Harker's igneous and metamorphic rock collection and catalogues were separated from the Sedgwick collections into the new Department of Mineralogy & Petrology. In 1931 too, A.G. Brighton became the first full-time curator of the Sedgwick Museum and over the next 38 years built up a huge manual catalogue of bound typescript supplemented by card indexes, annotated library volumes and archival material. This catalogue, though still intact, was superseded in 1983 by the present computer-based cataloguing system in which the complete catalogue is stored in machine readable form and is available on-line through a sophisticated information retrieval system. Complete hard-copy versions of the catalogue and a taxonomic index are generated periodically on microfiche.

Displays:

A large proportion of the collection is on permanent display in a fixed array of cases and as mounted vertebrate skeletons. Part of this display is intended to preserve the essentially Victorian/early Edwardian character of the early Sedgwick Museum. Such display also has the advantage of allowing students and the increasingly well-informed public readily to identify their own collected fossils by direct comparison. Other areas of the museum are, however, being re-vamped along more modern lines.

Research facilities:

All the facilities of a large, well-equipped Earth Sciences Department are available by arrangement with the curators or, in the case of major equipment needs such as electron microscopes, with the departmental administrator.

Staff:

Director, D.B. Norman BSc, PhD; Curators, G. Chinner PhD; R.B. Rickards, BSc, MA, PhD, ScD, FGS, C Geol; Conservator, C.J. Collins, BSc; Computer Officer, P. Phillips; Research Associate, N. Court PhD; Designer, C. Hall; Technical Staff, M.G. Dorling; S. Laurie; N. Payton; R.A. Long.

Other information:

Other Department of Earth Science collections include the John Watson Building Stone collection, the Maurice Black sedimentary rock collection, the Cambridge Spitsbergen Expedition collection, the N.F. Hughes palynomorph collection, the Alfred Harker igneous and metamorphic rock collection and the mineral museum (soon to be housed in a new gallery, the Whewell Gallery, contiguous with the Sedgwick collections). The Department's Bullard Laboratories (Geophysics), the Godwin Laboratories (Quaternary research), the Scott Polar Research Institute and the British Antarctic Survey are all nearby. The University Museum of Zoology has large collections of vertebrate fossils.

Compilers:

R.B. Rickards & D. Price.

EAST-CENTRAL AND SOUTH-EAST ENGLAND

COLCHESTER
Colchester Museums

Addresses:
Natural History Museum, High Street, Colchester, CO1 1DN. Telephone 0206 712941 [displays only]; 14 Ryegate Road, Colchester, CO1 1YG. Telephone 0206 712936 [Resource Centre].

Administration:
Colchester Borough Council.

Admission:
Free. School parties are advised to book through the main office (tel. 0206 712931/2) as numbers in the gallery area are controlled at peak periods.

Times of opening:
Tuesday - Saturday 10.00 - 13.00, 14.00 - 17.00.

History:

The geology collections date back to the middle of the last century and were part owned by Colchester Natural History Society and the Borough. They were originally displayed in their entirety in the museum in the old Norman Castle until about 1920 when they were placed in store or loaned to other organisations. The loan material, which was fully listed, was returned some years later and placed in store. The present Natural History Museum was opened in the former All Saints Church in the High Street in 1957 and the remains of the old collection were gradually transferred there. In recent years the reserve collections and library have been transferred to the Museum Resource Centre leaving only the new displays (opened 1991) in the High Street museum.

Principal collections:

J. Yelloly-Watson - minerals; J.B. Lott - coralline crag fossils; Sudbury Museum Collection; A.E. MacAndrew - copper & silver ores from South America; C.R. Bree - Pleistocene fossils; University of Chicago excavation - Clactonian fossils; British Natural History Society - Barton Bed molluscs; New Zealand Collection - Moa bones.

Major strengths:

Pleistocene mammals including material from the English Channel and local gravel deposits; Clactonian fossils.

Number of specimens:
c. 10,000; 1 figured, several referred.

Displays:
The small geology displays deal with the subject at a beginners level in the areas of the Ice Age, interglacials, Red Crag, London Clay, the Colchester Earthquake and the search for coal in Essex. There is a fossil wall with a diagrammatic section including real and replica fossils for "hands-on" use.

Research facilities:
Binocular microscope, small range of journals, books, offprints and maps mainly concerned with Cretaceous and Caenozoic, with particular reference to Essex.

Current projects:
Improvement of documentation and storage.

Staff:
Curator of Natural History, J.J. Heath, BA, AMA; Assistant Curator of Natural History, J.P. Bowdrey, BSc, AMA.

Compiler:
Jeremy Heath

EAST-CENTRAL AND SOUTH-EAST ENGLAND

DARTFORD
Dartford Borough Museum

Address:
Market Street, Dartford, DA1 1EU. Telephone 0322 343555; Fax 0322 343422.

Administration:
Dartford Borough Council.

Admission:
Free.

Times of opening:
Monday, Tuesday, Thursday, Friday 12.30 - 17.30, Saturday 09.00 - 13.00, 14.00 - 17.00. Extended opening hours during August.

History:
Dartford Museum was founded in 1908 to interpret the human and natural history of the Dartford area. The Museum moved into purpose-built premises in 1937 and was "modernised" in the mid-1950's, becoming a showpiece local history Museum. The Museum's current role is to highlight and interpret the history of the Borough of Dartford.

Principal collections:
E.E.S. Brown (c.1956); A.L. Leach (c.1928-1933); J.N. Carreck (c.1950's-1970's); R.H. Chandler (c.1905-1956); S. Priest (c.1939-1940); F.J. Epps (c.1928-1936); A.G. Wrigley; C.W. Wright; A.G. Davis (c. 1956); A.T. Marston (c.1938-1966); G.E. Dibley; J. Griffiths; W. Furner (c. 1907-1909).

Major strengths:
Cretaceous and Gault Clay fossils; north Kent fossils, rocks and minerals; Pleistocene material. Much of the material comes from localities no longer exposed, whilst other collections relate to localities such as Swanscombe which continue to be of high scientific interest.

Number of specimens:
c. 10,000.

Displays:
Small permanent display featuring some of the common local fossils and minerals.

Public services:
School loan service (including rocks, fossils and minerals); free object identification service; basic geological/palaeontological reference works.

Staff:
Curator, Peter W. Boreham, MA.

Compiler:
P.W. Boreham.

EAST-CENTRAL AND SOUTH-EAST ENGLAND

HASLEMERE
Haslemere Educational Museum

Address:
High Street, Haslemere, GU27 2LA. Telephone 0428 642112.

Administration:
The Museum is a private educational charity with voluntary Trustees and a Committee of Management.

Admission:
Adults £1.00; children (ages 5-14) £ 0.50. The Museum operates a membership scheme, an annual subscription of £5.00 (adults) allowing free admission to the Museum, a series of lectures and access to the attractive grounds as well as use of the extensive library. The Junior Club (annual subscription £1.00) meets on the first Saturday of each month for talks and demonstrations, and members qualify for discounts on tickets for holiday events.

Times of opening:
April - October: Tuesday - Saturday 10.00 - 17.00;
November - March: Tuesday - Saturday 10.00 - 16.00.
Closed Sundays and National Holidays.

History:

The Museum was founded in 1888 when Sir Jonathan Hutchinson, an eminent surgeon, set up a small private museum in out-buildings at his home an Inval, Haslemere. He had given much thought to the question of museum reform and introduced into his own institution a number of novel ideas, including the *Space for Time* schedules of geology and human history which, in a modified form, occupy an important part of the present displays.

Hutchinson, who founded two other museums in London and Selby, which closed soon after his death in 1913, built up substantial collections of natural history, geology and archaeology.

The Museum moved to its present building in 1926 and exhibition galleries were added to the side of the original Queen Anne house. The collection of European Peasant Art artefacts was transferred to the museum at this time. Other buildings added in the 1960's include a teaching laboratory as the Museum was becoming well-known for educational activities which are still offered to all age groups.

The Museum was the first actively to encourage school parties to visit and to introduce living specimens to the displays.

Principal collections:

J.E. Lee; J.C. Hawkshaw; G.F. Walton; A. Geike; A. Richards. The most notable is that of Sir Archibald Geikie, who retired to Haslemere and in 1914, following the death of Sir Jonathan Hutchinson, became the first Chairman of the Museum.

Archives:

Included with the collection of Sir Archibald Geikie (above) are his field notebooks, correspondence and an extensive collection of watercolours.

Major strengths:

The palaeontological collection includes examples of all the main invertebrate groups. It is particularly strong in echinoids, bivalves and Tertiary gastropods. The collection is also strong in material from the Chalk, Barton Beds and the Red Crag. Most of the material comes from localities in the south of England, but other British sites are represented along with overseas sites such as the Lebanon and Solenhofen, Germany.

The rock collection includes representatives of most rock types with south of England localities better represented than other British sites. There are some foreign specimens.

The mineral collection is comprehensive and contains examples of all the main mineral groups. It is particularly strong in heavy metals, agates and opals. It includes material from many localities world-wide, from Switzerland, America and Australia.

Number of specimens:

c. 10,000.

Displays:

The displays start with an explanation of how the planet was formed. This is followed by the *Space for Time* schedule. Along one wall geological time is represented by one foot to every 10 million years. Each geological period is illustrated with specimens and an environmental reconstruction. There are also displays of minerals and rocks.

Staff:

Curator, Diana M. Hawkes, BA.

Compiler:

D. Hawkes.

EAST-CENTRAL AND SOUTH-EAST ENGLAND

HITCHIN
North Hertfordshire Museums

Address:
Natural History Department, Museum Resource Centre, Burymead Road, Hitchin, SG5 1RT.
Telephone 0462 434476, ext. 2384.

Administration:
North Hertfordshire District Council.

Admission:
Free.

Times of opening:
Monday - Friday 10.00 - 17.00 by appointment.

History:

Founded 1914 by Letchworth Naturalists Society, taken over by Letchworth UDC in 1938, amalgamated with Hitchin Museum following local government reorganisation in 1974 to form North Hertfordshire Museums Service.

Major strengths:

Local Upper Cretaceous and Pleistocene material, particularly Chalk fossils and glacial erratics.

Number of specimens:

c. 10,000.

Displays:

Some geology included in Natural History displays at The Letchworth Museum, Broadway, Letchworth (open Monday - Saturday 10.00-17.00).

Research facilities:

Library and some research facilities.

Staff:

Countryside Officer, Brian Sawford.

Compiler:

B. Sawford.

William Hill with Hoxnian interglacial deposits in the Hitchin buried tunnel valley complex (c. 1885)

EAST-CENTRAL AND SOUTH-EAST ENGLAND

IPSWICH
Ipswich Museum

Address:
High Street, Ipswich, IP1 3QH. Telephone 0473 213761.

Administration:
Ipswich Borough Council, Leisure Services Department.

Admission:
Free.

Times of opening:
Tuesday - Saturday 10.00 - 17.00. Closed Bank Holidays.

History:

The Mechanics Institute and the Literary Institution both had museum rooms in the 1830's. Edward Charlesworth referred to fossil shark teeth in "Ipswich Museum" in the Magazine of Natural History in 1837. A purpose-built museum was opened in Museum Street in 1847 and included displays of geological specimens; Ipswich Corporation took over its running and funding in 1853. The Museum moved to the present High Street premises in 1881. Museum Presidents who have written on geological matters are John Stevens Henslow (1850-1861), Edwin Ray Lankester (1901-1929) and James Reid Moir (1929-1944); also Curator John Ellor Taylor (1872-1893) and Museum Assistant Harold E.P. Spencer (1925-1965).

Principal collections:

A. Bell - Red Crag molluscs; R. M. Brydone - Chalk fossils; H. Canham - Red Crag mammals; Miss Cautley - Sewalik Hills mammals; W. Crowfoot - Tertiary molluscs from France & Italy; C.G. Doughty - Red Crag molluscs; N.F. Layard - Upper Pleistocene mammals; R.A.D. Markham - Crag fossils; J.R. Moir - Pleistocene mammals; C. Morley - Crag molluscs; H.E.P. Spencer - Pleistocene mammals.

Archives:

Library with some older journals. Manuscript notes of A. Bell and J.R. Moir.

Major strengths:

Local Pliocene ("Crag") and Pleistocene molluscs and mammals; local Palaeolithic flints.

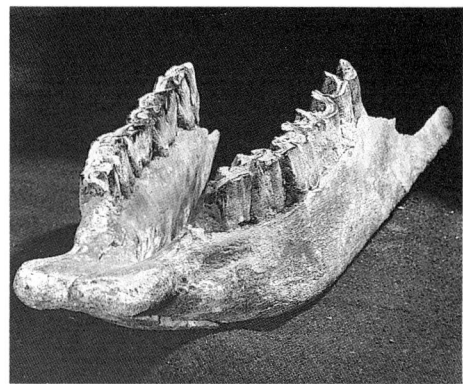
Woolly Rhinoceros from the Pleistocene of Ipswich

Number of specimens:
c.50,000; several type and many figured.

Publications:

Taylor, J.E. 1871. *A guide to the Ipswich Museum*. Ipswich Museum.

Bell, A. 1917. A list of type and figured specimens in the Geological Collection. *Journal of the Ipswich and District Field Club*.

Markham, R.A.D. 1968. An introduction to the Geological Collections of Ipswich Museum. *Bulletin of the Ipswich Geological Group*, **4**.

Markham, R.A.D. 1990. *A rhino in High Street - Ipswich Museum, the early years*. Ipswich Museum.

Displays:

Two Geology galleries with over 1,500 specimens on display. The *Rocks and Fossils* General Geology Gallery was re-displayed in 1983 and the *Suffolk Geology* Gallery in 1986.

Staff:

Keeper of Geology, R.A.D. Markham.

Other information:

Lectures and field excursions held regularly. Worksheets for younger visitors include *A day in the life of Lake Ipswich* (interglacial specimens trail).

Compiler:
R.A.D. Markham.

EAST-CENTRAL AND SOUTH-EAST ENGLAND

LONDON
Horniman Public Museum

Address:
100 London Road, Forest Hill, London SE23 3PQ.
Telephone 081 699 1872/2339/4911.

Administration:
Horniman Public Museum and Public Park Trust.

Admission:
Free.

Times of opening:
Monday - Saturday 10.30 - 18.00, Sunday 14.00 - 18.00. Closed Christmas.

History:

In 1901 Frederick Horniman presented the Museum with its collection and Gardens to the London County Council to encourage public interest in natural history, human culture and beliefs. He commissioned a purpose-built museum from the architect C. Harrison Townsend, which opened in 1904.

Principal collections:

Dalton Collection (c.5,500 specimens) - fossils; Arthur Wyatt Bequest (c.1,700) - minerals and fossils; W.H. Bennett Collection (c.75,000) - includes Burgess Shale fossils.

Major strengths:

Broad historical, international and stratigraphic coverage with palaeontological emphasis.

Number of specimens:

c.100,000.

Displays:

Dalton Fossil Collection on display in North Hall balcony.

Staff:

Keeper of Natural History, Jim Brock, PhD; Assistant Keeper of Natural History, L.A. Patrick; Temporary Assistant in Geology, Gordon Alchin.

Compiler:

L.A. Patrick.

EAST-CENTRAL AND SOUTH-EAST ENGLAND

LONDON
Natural History Museum: Department of Mineralogy

Address:
Cromwell Road, London, SW7 5BD. Telephone 071 938 9353; Fax 071 938 9268.

Admission:
Adults £5.00; children (ages 5-17) senior citizens, registered disabled, UB40 holders £2.50; family groups (up to 2 adults, 4 children) £13.50. Free Monday - Saturday 16.30 - 17.50, Sunday 17.00 - 17.50. Season ticket: (NHM only) Adult £9.00 ; Children (ages 5–17), senior citizens, registered disabled, UB40 holders £4.50; Family £25.00 . Season ticket (joint museums – V&A, NHM, Sci. Mus.): Adult £16.00; Children (ages 5–17) £7.50; Family £32.00.

Times of opening:
Monday - Saturday 10.00 - 17.50, Sunday 11.00 - 17.50.

History:
See below under Department of Palaeontology.

Principal collections:

Mineral Gallery, view looking east

Mineral Collection: The mineral collection is one of the finest of its type in the world. The 1753 acquisition by the nation of the extensive collection of Sir Hans Sloane, laid a foundation with a number of carved and decorative objects of precious and semi-precious materials. However, the first true mineral acquisitions were made in 1799 with 868 fine specimens from the collection of the Rev. Clayton Mordaunt Cracherode, and a further 7,000 purchased from the collection of Charles Hatchett in 1800. Other notable early additions were the collection of the Rt Hon. Charles Greville which included the historically important collection of Ignatz von Born in 1810, a collection of Brazilian minerals from Frederick Tendron also in 1810, various choice specimens purchased at the auction sales of Henry Heuland about 1836, 550 choice Cornish specimens from John Charles Williams MP, the collection of Thomas Allan and R.P. Greg in 1864, a large collection from Miss Caroline Birley in 1907, the Sir Arthur Church collection of cut gemstones in 1915 and the valuable collection of Swiss minerals from F.N.A. Fleischmann (later Ashcroft) in 1936. More recent additions include the most important collection of 12,000 British minerals from Sir Arthur Russell in 1964, and a similar number from Arthur Kingsbury in 1968, the Smith and Key purchase of 1,100 world class specimens in 1968, and the excellent collection of 128 Burmese gemstones of A.C.D. Pain in 1971. Most recently the merging of the Natural History Museum and the Geological Museum in 1985 has added an estimated 50,000 minerals and gemstones. The collection now contains an estimated 300,000 specimens and is seen as the major national research resource.

Gemstone Collection: Although not strictly kept as a separate collection, the merger in 1985 of the Natural History Museum and the Geological Museum added the latter's world-renowned collection of cut gemstones and gem materials to those already interspersed in the Natural History Museum mineral collection. The addition brings the number of cut stones in the combined collection up to about 5,000 and includes excellent examples of corundum, spinel, garnet, peridot and such rare items as taaffeite.

Ore Collection: Separate from the main mineral

collection is the ore collection, comprising individual specimens and suites from metalliferous mining areas chiefly in Britain, but also with significant world-wide representation. The collection has expanded significantly in the last decade with a number of specialised collecting trips and now contains an estimated 5,000 specimens. These include important suites from Cornwall, Devon, the Mendips, South Wales, the northern Pennines and Scotland. The collection provides valuable research material for metallogenesis studies. Several thousand more specimens, including valuable and unique suites from world-wide locations, have been added following the merger of the Natural History Museum and the Geological Museum in 1985. In addition to the specimens there is also a reference collection of nearly 2,000 polished ore-mounts.

Russell Collection: The collection of Sir Arthur Russell, 6th Baronet of Swallowfield Park, Reading, is internationally recognised as one of the greatest assembled private collections. It comprises some 12,000 specimens covering the whole of the British Isles and was bequeathed to the Department and nation along with mahogany cabinets and associated papers upon the death of Sir Arthur in 1964, on condition that it be kept separate as a regional collection. It is particularly strong in the species fluorite, calcite and baryte, all of which Sir Arthur was particularly fond, and additionally contains specimens from many old and historically important collections, including many specimens figured by Philip Rashleigh in his work on British minerals.

Ashcroft Collection: This collection of about 6,000 quality specimens from central Switzerland, was acquired over a period up to 1938 from F.N.A. Fleischmann (who later changed his name to Ashcroft), along with a unique photographic catalogue of collecting sites. It is acknowledged as one of the best collections of Swiss minerals and contains superb specimens of sphene, pink fluorite, hematite and twisted smoky quartz ("gwindel") groups, along with a number of rare species. The catalogue contains outstandingly clear photographs taken by Ashcroft of all the collecting sites, along with maps, lists of specimens obtained and examples of specimen labels, all contained in about 160 leather-bound spring binders.

Petrology Collection: The Hans Sloane Collection of some 500 clays, marbles and stones was acquired by the nation in 1753 although most of the early specimens have subsequently disappeared. This formed the basis for the Petrological Collection which now consists of some 250,000 specimens. Many collections from voyages of exploration and from parts of the British Empire were added; for a listing of these see Campbell-Smith, 1928. The major strengths are rocks from oceanic islands, alkaline igneous rocks and rocks from expeditions of exploration (J.C. Ross, Sir E. Shackleton, R. F. Scott, HMS Challenger, Terra Nova, Discovery and Quest etc.). With the recent merging of the Natural History Museum and the Geological Museum collections, 17,000 specimens of building and decorative stones were acquired together with the Geological Society collection of British rocks.

Meteorite Collection: The meteorite collection consisting of c. 3,200 specimens has been built up by small donations from individuals rather than the acquisition of whole collections. Sources as varied as The Lords Commissioners of the Admiralty, The Asiatic Society of Bengal and The Geological Survey of India are listed in a 1904 British Museum (Natural History) publication of the collections. Specimens were not displayed until the early 19th century since meteorites were not recognised as having an extra-terrestrial origin. A noteworthy addition to the collection was the gift of the 3.5 ton Cranbourne meteorite by James Bruce in 1862. This specimen, the largest in the collection, is on display in the Meteorite Pavilion at South Kensington. In 1959, a donation from the Nuffield Trust enabled the British Museum (Natural History) to purchase part (269 specimens) of the collection of H.H. Nininger. 325 specimens were acquired in the merger of the Natural History Museum and the Geological Museum in 1985.

Ocean Bottom Deposits Collection: The collection of over 30,000 samples of sea-bed deposits is founded on the famous "Challenger" collection which was donated to the Museum in 1921 following the death of Sir John Murray in 1914. Samples dating back to 1844 from the east coast of America and many from early trans-ocean cable ships form part of the Murray Collection. Most of the pre-1940 "Discovery" samples from the southern oceans are represented as well as the cores, nodules and sediments from the 1933-34 John Murray

Expedition to the Indian Ocean. Recent important additions include the University College, London collections of sediments from the West Indies and the Denis Curry collection of sediments from the English Channel. A large part of the post-1940 samples were collected by HM survey ships and have a world-wide distribution. The collection is at present housed away from the Museum in an outstation.

Number of specimens:

c.633,000 (see above).

Published catalogues:

Anon. 1971. *An index to the systematic collection of minerals in the British Museum (Natural History).* London.

Campbell Smith, W. 1928. *Catalogue of the rock collection in the Mineralogy Department of the British Museum (Natural History). Part 1, Africa.* British Museum (Natural History), London.

Campbell Smith, W. 1932. *Catalogue of the rock collection in the Mineralogy Department of the British Museum (Natural History). Part 2, America.* British Museum (Natural History), London.

Campbell Smith, W. and Game, P.M. 1954. *Catalogue of the rock collection in the Mineralogy Department of the British Museum (Natural History). Part 3, Antarctica and Australia.* British Museum (Natural History), London.

Bishop, A.C., Jones, V., Moore, D.T. & Woolley, A.R. 1971. *Catalogue of the rock collection in the British Museum (Natural History).* British Museum (Natural History), London.

Moore, D.T., Jones, V., Woolley, A.R. and Bishop, A.C. 1979. *Catalogue of chemically analysed igneous rocks in the British Museum (Natural History).* British Museum (Natural History), London.

Moore, D.T., Thackray, J.C. and Morgan, D.L. 1991. A short history of the Museum of the Geological Society of London, with an index of the British and Irish Geological accessions and a note on some Survey collections. *Bulletin of the British Museum (Natural History) (Historical Series),* **19**(1), 5/–160.

Graham, A.L., Bevan, A.R.W. and Hutchison, R. 1985. *Catalogue of meteorites with special reference to those represented in the collection of the British Museum (Natural History).* British Museum (Natural History), London.

Buckley, H.A., Elliott, C.J., Graham, N.M., Johnson, L.R., Kempe, D.R.C. and Williams, D.B. 1979. *Catalogue of Ocean Bottom Deposits Collection in the British Museum (Natural History). Part 1, Atlantic and Arctic Oceans including the European Seas.* British Museum (Natural History), London, 12 pp. [6 microfiches].

Buckley, H.A., Graham, N.M., Johnson, L.R., Kempe, D.R.C., Morgan, D.L. and Williams, D.B. 1984. *Catalogue of Ocean Bottom Deposits Collection in the British Museum (Natural History). Part 2, Indian and Pacific Oceans.* British Museum (Natural History), London, 4pp. [5 microfiches].

Kempe, D.R.C. and Buckley, H.A. 1987. Fifty years of oceanography in the Department of Mineralogy, British Museum (Natural History). *Bulletin of the British Museum (Natural History), (Historical series),* **15**, 59-97.

Displays:

The Mineral Gallery houses probably the world's finest extant systematic display of minerals. Upwards of 14,000 specimens are shown in table cases covering nearly 2,000 mineral species. Each species shows as wide a range of locality, colour, associated species, crystallography etc. as space and the range of specimens permits. Also there are wall cases each containing about 20 large and choice specimens including some of the world's finest examples. In addition to the systematic display there are displays showing an introduction to minerals, pseudomorphs, synthetic crystals, mineral properties and fluorescence, as well as selections from the collections of Sir Hans Sloane, A.C.D. Pain, Sir Arthur Russell and A.W.G. Kingsbury. The best of the former Geological Museum gemstone collection is still displayed in specially constructed cases on the ground floor of the Geological Museum building. A number of items of ore material can be found in metalliferous displays of the Geological Museum, displayed in a geographical and elemental order. A comprehensive exhibition of igneous, sedimentary and metamorphic rocks, arranged systematically, is displayed in the Mineral Gallery. Other displays include rock classification, rock forming minerals, weathering effects, pebbles, concretions and nodules, organic sediments and volcanoes. Housed in the Meteorite Pavilion are displays describing the origin and types of meteorites with examples of each.

Staff:

Keeper of Mineralogy, Paul Henderson, PhD; plus many research scientists, curatorial staff and technical specialists.

Compilers:

P. Tandy & H.A. Buckley.

EAST-CENTRAL AND SOUTH-EAST ENGLAND

LONDON
Natural History Museum: Department of Palaeontology

Address:
Cromwell Road, London, SW7 5BD. Telephone 071 938 9250; Fax 071 938 9277.

Admission:
Adults £5.00; children (ages 5–17), senior citizens, registered disabled, UB40 holders £2.50; Family groups (up to 2 adults, 4 children) £13.50. Free Monday–Saturday 16.30–17.50, Sunday 17.00–17.50. Season ticket (NHM only): Adult £9.00; children (ages 5–17), senior citizens, registered disabled, UB40 holders £4.50 ; Family £25.00. Season ticket (joint museums – V&A. NHM, Sci. Mus.): Adult £16.00; children (ages 5–17) £7.50; Family £32.00.

Times of opening:
Monday - Saturday 10.00 - 17.50, Sunday 11.00 - 17.50.

History:

The collections in the Natural History Museum stem from those of Sir Hans Sloane (1660-1753), who willed that the extensive collection of plants, animals, rocks, minerals, fossils, antiquities, scientific instruments and their associated library that he had accumulated at considerable expense during his life, should be acquired by the nation. These collections were transferred to Montagu House, Bloomsbury in June 1753 and became the foundation of the British Museum. The continued growth of the natural history collections resulted in the division of the Natural History Department during 1837 into the three branches of Botany, Zoology and Mineralogy & Geology. Despite the move to new buildings in Bloomsbury in 1845, the natural history collections had so outgrown the rest of the British Museum's holdings by 1856 that it was recognised that they required a separate organisation, and this led to the removal of the natural history material to the present site in South Kensington in 1881. The Geology Department's name was changed to Palaeontology in 1956 and the Natural History Museum became independent from the British Museum in 1963. A new East Wing to hold the Department of Palaeontology and its extensive collections was built in 1976. The prime purposes of the Department are curation and conservation of the collections and research upon them and on all relevant aspects of earth sciences.

Principal collections:
Important collections listed are C.D.E Konig (1825); the Sowerby family; G. Mantell (1838, 1853); W. Gilbertson (1841); T. Davidson (1886). The foreign material belonging to the Geological Survey was transferred in 1880 and that of the Geological Society in 1911. The specimens once belonging to members of the first London Clay Club: J.S. Bowerbank, N.T. Wetherell, John Morris and especially S.V. Wood and F.E. Edwards have ensured that the Tertiary collections are un-surpassed and the substantial collections of A.W. Wrigley and A.G. Davis have since been added to these. This century, the collections have grown through field work carried out in most areas of the world by staff of the Department and by many substantial donors, both professional and amateur, including many oil companies. Highlights include:

Arthropoda: Trilobita (>200,000 specimens): a diverse collection containing important material from Mrs Gray and F. Rasetti and new acquisitions from the Arctic and China; substantial collections of Crustacea from Europe, augmented by specimens from the Far East; also material described by T.H. Withers; also holds the most extensive series of fossil Insecta (>40,000) in the UK, including the Brodie material and a large amber collection.

Brachiopoda: (>300,000 specimens): historic material from the collections of J. Sowerby, T. Davidson (together with his notebooks), W. Gilbertson & S.S. Buckman; many other important collections, e.g. B.B. Bancroft, A. Williams, A.D. Wright.

Bryozoa: (5,000 type & figured specimens; c.1,000,000 specimens): includes the collections of W.D. Lang and J.W. Gregory and the important Cretaceous collections of C.T.A. Gaster and A.W. Rowe.

Corals, Stromatoporoids and Sponges: (200,000 specimens): the most important collections are those of H. Milne Edwards & J. Haime (British), R.I. Murchison (Russian Platform), P.M. Duncan (West Indies & British),

H.A. Nicholson, J.W. Gregory (India and elsewhere), S. Smith (Palaeozoic) and R.G.S. Hudson (Middle East).

Echinodermata: (>100,000 specimens): contains parts of several classical early collections including T. Wright, W. Gilbertson (Carboniferous crinoids), F. Dixon, G. Mantell and W. Smith; that were augmented by those of Mrs E. Gray (Palaeozoic), A.W. Rowe (British Cretaceous), S. Westhead (Carboniferous crinoids).

Graptolites: (c. 15,000 specimens): historical collections by H.A. Nicholson and others, plus more recent world-wide material.

Mollusca (Cephalopoda): (>200,000 specimens): an extensive world-wide collection from most geological ages, which apart from the historically important specimens of the Sowerbys, W. Gilbertson, J.E. Astier, and Tesson, contain material from W.D. Lang, S.S. Buckman and more recently W.J. Kennedy, J.M. Hancock and C.W. Wright.

Mollusca (Bivalvia & Gastropoda): (>3,000,000): in addition to those mentioned above, has material from many older European collections, e.g. Tesson, L.G. de Koninck, A.E.M. Cossman and G.P. Deshayes. Several significant collections of recent years have provided important Cretaceous material, e.g. W.J. Kennedy & C.W. Wright to enhance those of H.B. Blackmore, G.E. Dibley, A.W. Rowe and J.S. Gardiner. Similarly important Palaeozoic and Jurassic collections are held to the major holdings of Tertiary & Quaternary mollusca.

Micropalaeontology and Palynology: Including the major collections of Recent material made by Heron-Allen & Earland, since augmented by the Challenger Collection described by Brady (1884); the numerous fossil collections contain the important planktonic foraminifera upon which Blow based his zonation, and much oil company material, also the ostracods described by J.W. Neave and his colleagues.

Palaeobotany: Range from algae to fossilised wood and contain type material of Jurassic, Cretaceous described by Sir Albert Seward, T.M. Harris, H.H. Thomas and Tertiary plants used by E. Reid and M.E.J. Chandler initially and M.E. Collinson latterly; the Williamson collection of Carboniferous plants; the Rufford Wealden plants, and the G.F. Elliott collection of algae.

Reptilia and Amphibia: (30,000 specimens): historic specimens extremely well-represented, ranging from the ichthyosaurs and plesiosaurs of Mary Anning and Thomas Hawkins to the dinosaurs and other reptiles described by Richard Owen and Gideon Mantell. The collection of Permian and Triassic material from the Karroo is also of world-wide consequence. The collection of notable British and African material by staff have maintained the major position of these holdings.

Birds: with over 5,500 specimens amongst the finest in the world and containing the notable *Archaeopteryx lithographica* specimen acquired in 1862 and many other unique specimens from Britain, New Zealand and South America.

Fish: (c. 250,000 specimens): an unrivalled and diverse collection containing many historic and important specimens, particularly the collections of Sir Philip Egerton and the Earl of Enniskillen.

Mammalia: material obtained from the past British Empire are the most notable, these range from the Siwalik specimens from India and Pakistan to extinct marsupials from Australia; also represented are Darwin's South American specimens, Irish deer, American *Mastodon* and Pliocene mammalia from Samos.

Palaeoanthropology: c. 15,000 human skeletal specimens and casts. Notable specimens include the Swanscombe, Gibraltar and Broken Hill (Zimbabwe) skulls, and the Piltdown fraud.

Major strengths:

The collections are organised zoologically and botanically according to the various phyla and classes, and are further subdivided by a varied hierarchy of zoological, stratigraphical, or geographical criteria. There are now approximately 9 million separate curated units. The earliest scientifically recognisable specimens are those presented by Gustavus Brander in 1765 and subsequently used by D.C. Solander in 1766. The first major purchase of a fossil collection was that of William Smith's material in 1816. Apart from the widely used dinosaur specimens, the various fossils obtained by Charles Darwin on the *Beagle* voyage are probably the most prestigious. The Department's holdings of historical and classical monograph material are particularly strong, while many of the early collections made by expeditions to, and settlers in, various parts of the world have also ultimately been acquired, e.g. A.G. Bain (South Africa), Paul Strzelecki and Thomas Mitchell (Australia).

Number of specimens:

> 9,000,000 (see above).

Published catalogues:

Throughout the nineteenth century there were published numerous authoritative descriptive catalogues of most parts of the collections and these have become the standard references for many groups of fossils. Since 1977, the staff of the Department have undertaken the production of a series of Catalogues recording the type and figured material present in the collections, e.g. Mesozoic Ammonoidea, Fossil Crustacea (excluding Ostracoda), Fossil Cephalopoda, Trilobita, Fossil Echinodermata, Macrofossil Algae.

Displays:

In the main Museum galleries there are substantial exhibits of *Dinosaurs, Our Place in Evolution, Marine Reptiles* and *Origin of Species*. In the Earth Science galleries there are permanent exhibits on *British Fossils, Story of the Earth, Britain before Man* and other geological displays on minerals, gemstones and the exploitation of the earth's resources.

Research facilities:

The Micropalaeontological Laboratory has facilities for thin-sectioning both fossil and rock specimens; the Palynology Laboratory has a "clean" hydrofluoric facility for breaking down obdurate material. The main Palaeontology Laboratory has facilities for the development, preservation and replication of material including a separate laboratory for acid preparation and undertakes research technique development. The Department maintains a General Enquiry service providing identification of fossil specimens and advice during normal working hours on weekdays. It also undertakes commercial work on biostratigraphy and palaeontology.

Staff:

Keeper of Palaeontology, L.R.M. Cocks, DPhil, DSc; plus c.60 research scientists, curatorial staff and technical specialists.

Compilers:

L.R.M. Cocks & R.J. Cleevely.

EAST-CENTRAL AND SOUTH-EAST ENGLAND

LONDON
Passmore Edwards Museum

Address:
Romford Road, Stratford, London, E15 4BZ.
Telephone 081 534 2274/0276.

Administration:
Leisure Services Department, Newham Borough Council and Governors of the Newham Museum Service.

Admission:
Free.

Times of opening:
Wednesday - Friday 11.00 - 17.00, Saturday 13.00 - 17.00, Sunday, Bank Holidays 14.00 - 17.00.

History:
Established in the 1890's by the Essex Field Club as the Essex Museum of Natural History. Half funded by John Passmore Edwards M.P. of Salisbury, Wiltshire, the newspaper publisher and philanthropist. Opened by the Countess of Warwick in 1900. Voluntarily staffed until 1956 when an arrangement was made with West Ham Corporation (later to become London Borough of Newham) and the museum was renamed as the Passmore Edwards Museum. The museum is now managed by a governing body comprising the local authority, the Essex Field Club, the Museums Association and others.

Major strengths:
Extensive collections of rocks, fossils and minerals.

Number of specimens:
c.20,000.

Displays:
Geology is represented in the *Newham Landscape* Gallery of the museum and from time to time in temporary exhibitions.

Staff:
No geologist on staff.

Compiler:
Colin Plant.

EAST-CENTRAL AND SOUTH-EAST ENGLAND

NORTHAMPTON
Northampton Central Museum and Art Gallery

Address:
Guildhall Road, Northampton, NN1 1DP. Telephone 0604 39415.

Administration:
Northampton Borough Council.

Admission:
Free.

Times of opening:
Monday - Saturday 10.00 - 17.00, Sunday 14.00 - 17.00. Closed Christmas Day, Boxing Day, New Year's Day.

History:

Founded 1865. During its history the Museum has acquired several large collections of renown geologists. One of the most important was that of Spencer Compton, 2nd Marquis of Northampton, presented to the Museum along with original furniture and his geological library by his family in 1878. Lord Northampton was President of the Geological Society from 1820-1822 and President of the Royal Society from 1838-1848. Many of his specimens were figured by Sir Roderick Murchison, Gideon Mantell and other pioneers.

The nucleus of the Museum's early geological collection was formed from a donation by one of its founders and Hon. Curators, Samuel Sharp. His collections were figured in early Palaeontographical Society monographs and included specimens from Dr Henry Porter's Collection. Specimens from the collections of other well-known local geologists and researchers, including John F. Bentley, Rev. A.W. Griesbach, T.J. George and Walter Drawbridge Crick, were added to the general museum collection. In 1892 the museum purchased most of Thomas Jesson's Northamptonshire material including fish figured by A.S. Woodward.

Another major purchase in 1922 was the stratigraphical collection of W. Beeby Thompson (1848-1931), a gifted and energetic local geologist and consultant petroleum engineer. This magnificent collection, meticulously documented, contains the most comprehensive stratigraphical record of the county's underlying Jurassic rocks and was considered to hold some of the best Lias material in the country.

Over the last fifty years, due to lack of resources, the collection has not received the treatment it deserves. Since the 1970's its deteriorating state became the subject of serious concern to many geologists. However, following the results of a collection survey in 1991, a rescue curation programme commenced in the autumn of 1992. Although the collection has suffered neglect, it is still one of the finest and most important geological collections in the Midlands.

Principal collections:

The Marquis of Northampton's collection comprises around 10,000 minerals and fossils. It is of world-wide provenance with particularly well represented material from Sicily, Italy and the Solenhofen Limestone of Bavaria. A majority of specimens are British and come from classic nineteenth century localities including Christian Malford, Stonesfield, Whitby, Lyme Regis and Warminster. Invertebrate fossil groups are well represented, particularly Devonian corals, Silurian and Permian trilobites, crustaceans, ammonites, *Coleoidea*, Cretaceous asteroids and Tertiary molluscs. The mineral collection of around 2,500 specimens contains rare samples of crocoite and vauquelinite from Beresk in the Ural Mountains of Russia.

The other major collection, the Beeby Thompson Collection, contains over 16,000 British fossils and rocks, arranged in stratigraphic order and spanning the whole geological column, but with a majority from local Jurassic sites. There is an emphasis on Lias and Cornbrash fossils, including bivalves, gastropods and reptiles. The collection contains type and figured material.

A number of important named collections have been incorporated into the general museum collection. These include Northamptonshire and Lincolnshire Jurassic fossils from Samuel Sharp; Cornbrash and Tertiary molluscs from Rev. A.W. Griesbach; fish and reptiles of Henry Porter; Great Oolite fossils of John Bentley; fossils, including mammals and bryozoans, from former Hon. Curator, Thomas J. George, and a small collection of gastropods and foraminifera mounted on slides from W.D. Crick. Although the main part of the Crick Collection is held by the Northamptonshire Natural History Society, the Museum's collection contains many type specimens, particularly gastropods. The Jesson Collection of local Jurassic and Cretaceous fossils includes some fine and important specimens, especially those from the Great Oolite and Oxford Clay.

The geological collection also holds a number of historic borehole core samples from Orton, Northampton and Gayton, and a small collection of Northamptonshire building stones assembled in 1989 by Dr Diana Sutherland of Leicester University.

Archives:

Archives related to Lord Northampton's Collection include a catalogue of minerals compiled by Dr R.J. King (c. 1972), a list of vertebrates compiled by J.B. Delair (1973) and a list of type, figured and cited specimens compiled by H. Torrens and J.A. Cooper. Archives also include a modern inventory of A. Beeby Thompson Collection compiled by Brian Webster and a building stone list by D.J. Sutherland (1989). Beeby Thompson's collection of annotated publications, manuscripts, maps and correspondence are preserved in the Local Room of Northampton Public Library.

Major strengths:

Northamptonshire fossils and rocks, particularly from the Middle Lias. The Beeby Thompson Collection is of inestimable value due to its high standard of documentation. The strengths of Lord Northampton's Collection are the polished Devonian corals and the beautifully preserved belemnites and ammonites from the Oxford Clay of Christain Malford, Wiltshire.

Number of specimens:

40,000 fossils, 2,500 minerals, 500 rocks; 84 type, figured and referred specimens have so far been identified.

Publications:

Cooper, J.A. 1974. Geological collections and collectors of note: Northampton Central Museum. *Newsletter of the Geological Curators' Group* **1**:2, 40-45. (With Appendix by H.S. Torrens)

Displays:

Currently there are no geological specimens on display.

Public services:

Activities for school parties using a small handling collection. Lecture theatre within the Museum. Identification and other enquiries dealt with on request. Collection available for research on written permission.

Compiler:

Rosemary Roden.

EAST-CENTRAL AND SOUTH-EAST ENGLAND

NORWICH

Norwich Castle Museum

Address:
Castle Meadow, Norwich, NR1 3JU. Telephone 0603 223644.

Administration:
Norwich Castle Museum is the headquarters and main museum of the Norfolk Museums Service which is responsible to a joint committee comprising Norfolk County Council and all the district councils within Norfolk.

Admission:
Adults £1.60; concessions £1.20; children £0.60.

Times of opening:
Monday - Saturday 10.00 - 17.00, Sunday 14.00 - 17.00.

History:

The museum was founded in 1825 as the private Norfolk and Norwich Museum and was originally in the Haymarket, Norwich. Having outgrown these premises in 1833 the museum briefly moved to Exchange Street, but moved again in 1838 to Museum Court, St Andrews Street, where it remained until 1894. From 1840 the general public were admitted. In 1893 the collections were handed over to the City of Norwich and moved to Norwich Castle, which until 1887 had served as the county gaol. Norwich Castle Museum was officially opened in 1894. In 1974, the Norfolk Museums Service was established as part of local government reorganisation. The nucleus of the geological collections dates from the mid-nineteenth century.

Principal collections:

Samuel Woodward (1790-1838); C.B. Rose (1790-1872); John King (c. 1800-1879); Anna Gurney (first half of 19th century); John Gunn (1801-1890); Robert Fitch (1802-1895); R.M. Brydone (1873-1943). Major collections have been donated recently by P. Whittlesea (Chalk) and J. Lightwing (Pleistocene mammals). In the last few years much Pleistocene vertebrate material has been obtained by staff fieldwork.

Major strengths:

Major collections of Pleistocene mammals (c. 7,000 specimens) from the Cromer Forest Bed Formation (early Middle Pleistocene), river valley deposits (mainly Upper Pleistocene) and crags (Lower Pleistocene) of East Anglia; Norfolk Chalk and other Cretaceous fossils (c. 10,000 specimens); Crag molluscs.

Number of specimens:

250,000.

Displays:

The geology gallery includes a general introduction to minerals, rocks and fossils and a display of minerals, rocks and fossils arranged stratigraphically from Cambrian to Pleistocene. Particular emphasis is given to Norfolk Cretaceous and Pleistocene fossils. Temporary displays in the Museum entrance gallery and in the ecology gallery include recent finds of Pleistocene vertebrates from gravel workings and from the Cromer Forest Bed.

Research facilities:

Binocular microscopes, extensive library, including older literature on East Anglia; good comparative osteological collection.

Current projects:

Collection of Pleistocene vertebrate material from Shropham, Norfolk. Excavation, conservation, research and display of unique elephant skeleton from the Cromer Forest Bed Formation.

Staff:

Assistant Keeper of Natural History, A.J. Stuart, BSc, PhD.

Compiler:

A.J. Stuart.

EAST-CENTRAL AND SOUTH-EAST ENGLAND

OXFORD
Oxford University Museum

Address:
Parks Road, Oxford, OX1 3PW. Telephone 0865 272950.

Administration:
University of Oxford, Committee for the Scientific Collections.

Admission:
Free.

Times of opening:
Monday - Saturday 12.00 - 17.00. Access for research visitors, schools and other parties by arrangement at other times. Closed Sunday, for a number of days over Christmas, and three days before Easter.

History:
The collections of the Oxford University Museum are based on the natural history specimens belonging to J. Tradescant (1587-1638) and his son J. Tradescant (1608-1662). The latter passed his private collection to Elias Ashmole (1617-1692), who presented it, together with his own ethnographic and other collections, to the University in 1677. They were initially housed in the original Ashmolean Museum (now the Museum of History of Science) which opened in 1683 and was devoted to the teaching of natural sciences. The first Keeper was Robert Plot (1640-1696), who wrote *A natural history of Oxfordshire* in 1677, with illustrations of fossils and minerals. His successor, Edward Lhwyd (1660-1709), published a catalogue of the mineral and fossil collections in 1699, from which specimens still survive. The present University Museum building was opened in 1860 and is a three-storey Neo-Gothic building that originally housed all the university science departments as well as the Radcliffe Science Library. It now houses the University's Entomological, Geological, Mineralogical and Zoological collections, which together rank second only to the National Collections.

Principal collections:
Palaeontological: William Buckland (1784-1856); John Phillips (1800-1874) - Yorkshire Carboniferous and Oxfordshire Jurassic; Sir Charles Lyell (1791-1875) - Tertiary molluscs of

The Museum Court

Europe and North America; T. and C.F.B. Hawkins - Lias reptiles; R.B. Grindrod (1811-c.1880) - Lower Palaeozoic of Welsh Borderlands; Miss E. Philpot (1780-1857) - fish etc. from Lyme Regis; W.J. Arkell (1904-1958) - Jurassic. The collections of J. Parker of Oxford and E.A. Walford of Banbury are foremost amongst the important suites of Oxfordshire fossils made by 19th century amateurs.

Mineralogical: These are second only to those of the National Collections, comprising in excess of 28,000 mineral specimens, 1,100 polished slabs of marble and other ornamental stones, approximately 250 meteorite specimens and thin sections, and approximately 250 gemstones. The principal collections are those of Dr R. Simmons (1782-1846); S. Jarrett - Corsi marble collection (1828); S.C. Marsh (1896); E. Roscoe (1908); Sir Ford North (1909); Dr H. Muller (1915); M.W. Thomas (1984).

Archives:
The archives of William Smith, John Phillips, William Buckland and others are of national importance.

Major strengths:

Palaeontological: Lower Palaeozoic shelly faunas (e.g. Llandovery research collections of 16,000 specimens, made by L.R.M. Cocks and A.M. Ziegler in the 1960's), Jurassic vertebrates (e.g. Liassic fish described by Agassiz; the Stonesfield, Bathonian, mammal fauna; Oxfordshire dinosaurs), Jurassic invertebrates (especially the mollusca monographed by W.J. Arkell), Cretaceous invertebrates (especially ammonites and collections from stratotype localities), Pleistocene vertebrates (especially the cave faunas described by Buckland, and the "Red Lady of Paviland", the most complete human skeleton known from the British Palaeolithic), plus important historical collections of Buckland, Phillips, MacCulloch, and Lyell.

Mineralogical: British and Central European minerals plus the Corsi "marble" collection.

Number of specimens:

>500,000 specimens; >700 types, >4,000 figured, many referred.

Published catalogues:

Anon. 1982. *Catalogue of meteorites*. Oxford University Museum.

Displays:

The museum houses entomological, geological, mineralogical and zoological displays in galleries, arcades and a central court. The geological displays are: *Geology of Oxfordshire*, 60m^2; *History of Life*, 88m^2; teaching displays on fossil invertebrates, 20m^2. In the central court, 230m^2 are occupied by displays of fossil vertebrates including dinosaurs - a cast of *Iguanodon bernissartensis* and skeletons of *Megalosaurus bucklandi, Cetiosaurus oxoniensis, Eustreptospondylus oxoniensis* and *Camptosaurus prestwichii*.

The mineralogical displays encompass a floor area of about 170m^2 with 76 cases displaying over 1,600 specimens of 600 species of minerals, plus the Corsi Marble Collection. The fabric of the museum also constitutes a geological display of British ornamental building stones, the floors and walls and 126 pillars of the interior including nearly as many different types, selected by John Phillips, the first curator of the museum.

Research facilities:

An infra-red spectrometer and a range of microscopes, rock saws, mechanical and chemical preparation facilities is available on site, as is a well-equipped photographic suite. The museum is adjacent to the Department of Earth Sciences, which has a wide range of facilities (electron microprobe, scanning electron microscope, X-ray fluorescence, mass spectrometers, X-ray, chemical, optical and thin-section laboratories, etc.). The museum has an extensive library, particularly strong in the field of Jurassic geology (the bequest of the late W.J. Arkell), and is close to both the Earth Sciences and University Science Libraries.

Current projects:

Revision of the geological displays, begun in 1976, were completed in 1988. Long-term projects under way are completing specimen and archive catalogues. Current mineralogical projects are new displays illustrating minerals and light, gemstones, decorative stones, fluorescence and historical topics.

Staff:

Curator of the Mineralogical Collections and Principal Curator, F.B. Atkins, MA, DPhil; Assistant Curator of the Mineralogical Collections, M.T. Price, MSc, AMA; Curator of the Geological Collections, W.J. Kennedy, MA, BSc, PhD, DSc, FGS; Assistant Curator of the Geological Collections, H.P. Powell, MA, AMA; Assistant Curator of the Geological Collections, D.J. Siveter, BSc, PhD.

Other information:

Other geological resources in close proximity include the Department of Earth Sciences (Curators are also University Lecturers and full teaching members of the Department), contiguous with the University Museum, which has full research facilities and extensive rock and thin-section collections, notably those of L.R. Wager (1904-1965).

Compilers:

F.B. Atkins, W.J. Kennedy, H.P. Powell.

EAST-CENTRAL AND SOUTH-EAST ENGLAND

PETERBOROUGH
Peterborough City Museum and Art Gallery

Address:
Priestgate, Peterborough, PE1 1LF. Telephone 0733 343329.

Administration:
Peterborough City Council, Leisure Services Department.

Admission:
Free.

Times of opening:
Tuesday - Saturday 10.00 - 17.00. Closed Christmas Day, Boxing Day, Good Friday and New Year's Day.

History:

The Museum was founded in 1881 by Peterborough Museum Society, but control was passed to Peterborough City Council in 1969. The building itself is an early nineteenth century Georgian-style townhouse, which was first occupied by the Museum collections in 1929.

Principal collections:

Burghley Collection (c.1,000 rocks, minerals and fossils).

Major strengths:

Collections relating to Peterborough area; local brick pit fossils especially Oxford Clay vertebrates (including the holotype of *Ophthalmosaurus monocharactus* Appleby); Jurassic rocks; Jurassic reptiles; Jurassic fish; Pleistocene mammals; Killer Whale skeleton from Bronze Age silts.

Number of specimens:

c.8,000.

Published catalogues:

Cross, T. 1975. *A catalogue of the fossil vertebrates in the City Museum, Peterborough, Part 1, Reptiles and Fish.* Peterborough City Museum & Art Gallery, 21pp.

Displays:

Geology and Wildlife Gallery (opened 1989) depicts the Peterborough area and its wildlife at

The Geology and Wildlife Gallery

three stages of geological history: first the Jurassic seas, with ammonites, belemnites, bivalves and brachiopods displayed together with Oxford Clay faunas which include some fine marine reptiles and fish; secondly the Ice Age, with gravel pit specimens of reindeer, red deer, bison, hippopotamus etc.; and finally the present day. Also the Dogsthorpe Pliosaur, discovered in 1990 and displayed in its entirety.

Staff:

First Assistant Curator (Natural Sciences), Gordon R. Chancellor, PhD, AMA.

Compiler:

M.D. Howe.

EAST-CENTRAL AND SOUTH-EAST ENGLAND

PORTSMOUTH

Portsmouth Natural Science Museum and Aquarium

Address:
Cumberland House, Eastern Parade, Southsea, Portsmouth, PO4 9RF. Telephone 0705 827261.

Administration:
Portsmouth City Council, Libraries, Museums & Arts Committee.

Admission:
Summer: adults £1.00; senior citizens £0.75; children (over 13), students £0.60; children (under 13) free; family rate (2 adults, 2 children) £2.60. Low season: adults £0.75; senior citizens £0.55; children (over 13), students £0.45; children (under 13) free; family rate (2 adults, 2 children) £1.95.

Times of opening:
Daily 10.30 - 17.30. Closed Christmas Eve, Christmas Day, Boxing Day.

History:
In 1931 Cumberland House was opened as a Natural History Museum and Art Gallery, but was requisitioned during World War II and the best part of the collections removed to the Old Guildhall, which was destroyed in March 1941. The losses included material collected by J. St John Burton from Barton-on-Sea and by J.F. Jackson (Hon. Curator, Sandown Museum). Cumberland House was re-opened in 1951, housing the entire museum collections until 1968/9. Since 1972 it has been exclusively devoted to Natural History.

Principal collections:
Collection of H.L.F. Guermonprez (1854-1924), a noted west Sussex naturalist; J. Turner Collection (mainly Tertiary).

Major strengths:
Cretaceous and Tertiary fossils.

Number of specimens:
c.10,000.

Displays:
The museum now has displays telling the story of the natural environment of Portsmouth from the time of the oldest rocks encountered in the Portsdown Borehole (200 m.y. ago) to the present.

Staff:
Assistant Keeper (Geology), T.A. Getty.

Compiler:
T.A. Getty.

EAST-CENTRAL AND SOUTH-EAST ENGLAND

READING
Reading Museums Service

Address:
The Museum of Reading, Town Hall, Blagrave Street, Reading, RG1 1QH. Telephone 0734 399800; Fax 0734 566719.

Administration:
Reading Borough Council, Contract Services: Theatres and Museums.

Admission:
Free.

Times of opening:
Tuesday - Saturday 10.00 - 17.00, Sunday 14.00 - 17.00.

History:
The Museum was founded in 1882 and opened to the public the following year.

Principal collections:
General Bayley Collection - mainly Russian minerals; Franklyn Jones Collection - local fossils.

Major strengths:
Small collections dealing with British stratigraphy and petrology; a larger world-wide mineral collection, including many from Russia; local fossils.

Number of specimens:
c.9,000.

Displays:
Re-opened (first stage) in September 1993. Future stages will include sections on geology considered as part of the region's natural environment.

Staff:
Keeper of Natural History, H. Carter.

Compiler:
H. Carter.

EAST-CENTRAL AND SOUTH-EAST ENGLAND

SAFFRON WALDEN
Saffron Walden Museum

Address:
Museum Street, Saffron Walden, CB10 1JL.
Telephone 0799 510333; Fax 0799 516550.

Administration:
Collections and buildings owned by Saffron Walden Museum Society, leased to Uttlesford District Council, who are responsible for management and administration.

Admission:
Adults £1.00; discounts £0.50; children (under 18) free. Season ticket £3.00; discounts £1.50.

Times of opening:
April - October: Monday - Saturday 10.00 - 17.00, Sunday & Bank Holidays 14.30 - 17.00; November - March: Tuesday - Saturday 11.00 - 16.00.

History:
Saffron Walden Natural History Society established the museum in 1832. It moved into its present building and opened in 1835.

Principal collections:
Edward Charlesworth (1813-1893); British Natural History Society (1848-1870's); John Brown (1780-1859); G.S. Gibson (c. 1880's); Mrs G.S. Gibson (1885); Rogers' Collection; R.B. Alexander; J. Smith; G.N. Maynard; Alicia Barker; Wyatt George Gibson; Iabez Gibson; Edmund Gibson; J.E. Foster Esq.; W.F. Tuke; W.M. Jukes; Richard Cornwallis Neville; Professor J.S. Henslow (1796-1881); Rev. Thomas Hopkins; Rev. Bree; Leathe's Collection; Sir Richard Owen KCB FRS (1804-1892); Thomas Hawkins FGS; Ernest Westlake FGS (1856-1922); Sir J. McAdam; Sir John St Aubyn (1758-1839); Brown Son and Maw of London; Robert Henson (1814-1864); William Fenwick; Royal College of Surgeons; Rev. J.W. Kenworthy; Sudbury Museum Collection; A. Midgley; Mr D. Dix; G. Nell; C.K. Probert; R.M. Christy; Mr Walton; J.J. Green; Rev. W.F.G. Pigott; Lord C. Harvey; W.H. Rolfe FSA; Captain L. Bliss; Mr S. Wilkes.

Number of specimens:
c. 5,000.

Published catalogues:
A catalogue was published in 1845, containing reference to the geological collections.

Displays:
A new geology gallery, emphasising local geological formations opened in 1993.

Education:
Loan boxes of fossils and minerals are available for local schools. Facilities for education currently being developed in conjunction with local advisory teachers.

Staff:
Curator, Len Pole; Natural Sciences Curatorial Officer, Nick Gordon.

Compiler:
L.M. Pole.

EAST-CENTRAL AND SOUTH-EAST ENGLAND

ST ALBANS
Museum of St Albans

Address:
Hatfield Road, St Albans, Hertfordshire, AL1 3RR.
Telephone 0727 819340.

Administration:
St Albans City and District Council.

Admission:
Free.

Times of opening:
Monday - Saturday 10.00 - 17.00, Sunday 14.00 - 17.00.

History:

The Hertfordshire County Museum was founded in St Albans in 1898 by Sir John Evans, an eminent archaeologist, and A.E. Gibbs, a keen entomologist. Subscribers set up a fund to build the museum, and the land in Hatfield Road was given by Lord Spencer. The original aims were to show the archaeology, geology, natural history, agriculture and technology of Hertfordshire.

Principal collections:

John Morrison FGC (d. 1912); James Saunders (1839-1925); W. Whitaker FGS (1836-1925); C.P. Chatwin; Sir G. Fordham (1854-1929); W.H. Fordham (1926-1961); Dr R.J. Leiper; G.A. Bullen; Dr Butler; John Hopkinson FGS (1844-1914); Sedgwick Museum (c.1900).

Major strengths:

Hertfordshire fossils from the Chalk, Cambridge Greensand and London Clay.

Number of specimens:

c. 5,000 fossils, c. 300 minerals, c. 100 rocks; few referred fossils, including Cretaceous fish.

Displays:

None.

Staff:

Keeper of Natural Sciences, David Curry, CBiol, MIBiol, DipEd Tech.

Compiler:

David Curry.

Hertfordshire Pudding Stone

EAST-CENTRAL AND SOUTH-EAST ENGLAND

SANDOWN
Museum of Isle of Wight Geology

Address:
High Street, Sandown, Isle of Wight, PO36 8AF.
Telephone 0983 404344.

Administration:
Isle of Wight County Council.

Admission:
Free.

Times of opening:
Monday - Friday 09.30 - 17.30, Saturday 09.30 - 16.30. Open Bank Holidays.

History:

Collections began in early 19th century and moved to the Library at Sandown in 1913. One of the most notable curators was J.F. Jackson who collected generally and particularly in the Chalk. Collections were redisplayed in 1985.

Major strengths:

Collections restricted to local material; dinosaurs; Pleistocene mammals; Palaeogene mammals; reptiles; Cretaceous invertebrates, especially nautiloids and ammonites.

Number of specimens:

>20,000.

Publications:

Dinosaur island (1990); *South-west coast* (1987); *Culver Cliff* (1987); *Whitecliff Bay* (1987); *Shanklin* (1987); *Reptiles on the rocks* (1978); *Museum of IOW geology* (1985).

Displays:

Modern displays of local geology, dinosaurs and other local fossils.

Staff:

Curator, Steve Hutt; Assistant Curator, Jon Radley.

Other information:

The museum acts as the Geological Locality Records Centre for the Isle of Wight. Extensive and flexible programme of educational field trips for students.

Lower Greensand Ammonites from the collection of Mr Paul Newton

Compiler:

S.C. Hutt.

EAST-CENTRAL AND SOUTH-EAST ENGLAND

WINCHESTER
Hampshire County Council Museums Service

Addresses:
Chilcomb House, Chilcomb Lane, Bar End, Winchester, SO23 8RD. Telephone 0962 846304.

[Hampshire County Council Museums Service includes: Andover Museum, Church Close, Andover, SP10 1DP; The Curtis Museum & Allen Gallery, High Street, Alton, GU34 1BA; Eastleigh Museum, The Citadel, 25 High Street, Eastleigh, SO5 5LF; Fareham Museum, Westbury Manor, 84 High Street, Fareham, PO16 0JJ; Gosport Museum, Walpole Road, Gosport, PO12 1NS; Havant Museum, East Street, Havant, PO9 1BS; The Red House Museum, Quay Road, Christchurch, BH23 1BU; The Willis Museum, Old Town Hall, Basingstoke, RG21 1QD.

Administration:
Hampshire County Council, Recreation Committee.

Admission:
Free (seasonal charges at some museums).

Times of opening:
Tuesday - Saturday 10.00 - 17.00. [Check individual museums for variations.]

History:
Geological collections at Alton Museum were initiated by William Curtis (1803-1881) who founded the Mechanics Institute in 1837 and the Museum in 1855. The Willis Museum was founded in 1931 by George Willis (1877-1970), and the Red House Museum founded by Herbert Druitt (1876-1943).

Principal collections:
Curtis; Willis; Druitt.

Major strengths:
Palaeontology of Hampshire, especially Upper Greensand, Chalk and Eocene.

Number of specimens:
c. 10,000.

Displays:
Local geology displays at most of the local museums. New geology display at Gosport Museum.

Plate VIII from Fossilia Hantoniensia, Gustavo Brander 1766

Research facilities:
Reference collection of books, periodicals, papers and offprints. Photocopying facilities are available at HQ and at the museums.

Current projects:
Site documentation, collection of research material and production of educational resources.

Staff:
Geologists, David Kemp, Tony Cross.

Other information:
The Museum Service acts as the Geological Locality Records Centre for Hampshire and convenes the Hampshire Geology Forum which co-ordinates the RIGS scheme in the county. Other geological resources in close proximity include the Geology departments of Southampton University and Portsmouth University.

Compiler:
Tony Cross.

EAST-CENTRAL AND SOUTH-EAST ENGLAND

WISBECH
Wisbech and Fenland Museum

Address:
Museum Square, Wisbech, PE13 1ES. Telephone 0945 583817.

Administration:
The Wisbech and Fenland Museum was founded as a Society in 1835. Since 1962, however, it has been a Charitable Trust; approximately two-thirds of the running costs are met by the Fenland District Council.

Admission:
Free. School parties should preferably book in advance. Guided tours £5.

Times of opening:
May - September: Tuesday - Saturday 10.00 - 17.00; October - April: Tuesday - Saturday 10.00 - 16.00.

History:

Founded as a Society in 1835. Appointed first professional Curator, the zoologist Thomas William Foster in 1841. Moved into present purpose-built premises in 1847. Amalgamated with Wisbech Literary Society and Wisbech Literary Institute in 1868. Saved from dissolution in 1925. Requisitioned by the ARP during Second World War. Set up as a charity in 1962.

Principal collections:

J.W. Bodger; E. Charlesworth (1813-1893) - Lower Eocene from Isle of Wight; I. Deck FGS (1795-1853); Gen. T. Hardwicke FRS, FLS (1763-1875); Rev. H. Fardell (1795-1854); Prof. O. Heer - Miocene plants and insects from Oenigen and Lausanne; H.M. Lee; G.A. Mantell FGS (1790-1852); C. Moore; A. Peckover (1803-1893); A. Peckover FRGS, FSA (b.1870); D. Peckover (1798-1867); W. Peckover FSA (1790-1873); C.B. Rose (1790-1872); Rev. J.G. Rutter 1856-1930 - Wiltshire fossils; S. Smith (1802-1892); Dr W. Stanger (1812-1854) - minerals from Scotland, Nigeria, Antigua and South Africa, plus fossil fish from Scotland and Stonesfield Slate pterosaurs; C.H. Townshend (1798-1868) - Eocene fish from Monte Bolca; J.E. Weatherhead; Dr Whitsted (d.1862); Rev. W.E. de Winks.

"Rocks and Fossils – the Pleistocene'"

Archives:

Many old collections have original documentation. Collection of Victorian models of "Ancient Monsters", apparently similar to those shown at the Crystal Palace Great Exhibition.

Major strengths:

The collections are mostly very early and some from sites no longer available. Much of the collection is from the Fens.

Number of specimens:

c.32,000; few status specimens.

Displays:

The new displays were designed by Cheryl Butler and Simon Timberlake of AMSSEE in 1988 to 1991 and constructed by the museum staff. They were officially opened in May 1992. Subjects covered include Ichthyosaurs; Geology of the Fens; Geological Timescale; Local Geology (Jurassic, Cretaceous, Pleistocene, Industry and Land Use); Invertebrate Fossils; Fish (Devonian, Lower Carboniferous, Permian, Jurassic, Eocene);

Stonesfield Slate; Geological Collectors; Ancient Monsters; Minerals.

Current projects:

A programme of computer cataloguing using MODES has begun and it is hoped to rationalise geological storage in the near future.

Staff:

Curator and Librarian, David C. Devenish, BA, AMA.

Other information:

The Museum is situated next to the Castle which is an educational centre with non-geological displays. Other geological resources in close proximity include the Sedgwick Museum and Peterborough Museum.

Compiler:

David C. Devenish.

WEST-CENTRAL AND SOUTH-WEST ENGLAND

BRISTOL

Bristol City Museum and Art Gallery

Address:
Queen's Road, Bristol, BS8 1RL. Telephone 0272 223592; Fax 0272 222047.

Administration:
Bristol City Council, Leisure Services Directorate.

Admission:
£2 (concessions £1). Bristol Leisure Card Holders, children under 16 and full-time students free.

Times of opening:
Daily 10.00 - 17.00. Check Bank Holidays with museum.

History:

Founded in 1823 as the museum of the Bristol Institution for the Advancement of Science, Literature and the Arts; transferred in 1894 to the City Council, and in 1905 became the Bristol Museum and Art Gallery. Present building completed in 1905 and extended in 1930. Curators during nineteenth and early twentieth centuries included J.S. Miller, Samuel Stutchbury, Robert Etheridge, William Sanders, W.J. Sollas, E.B. Tawney, Edward Wilson, Herbert Bolton and F.S. Wallis.

On 24th November 1940 the geological gallery was destroyed in an air raid, and all the exhibits and reference collections in it were lost.

Principal collections:

The largest collections are those of J. Chaning Pearce, H.S. Torrens, J.W. Tutcher and T.R. Fry, all particularly strong in Jurassic material of the west of England. Chief mineral collections include R.P. Wild and B.V. Cooper. Other collections include A. Bentley, G.W. Braikenridge, R. Bright, C.J.T. Copp, J. Cottle, G. Hope Dixon, Earl of Ducie, H.F. Fermor, W. Gazy, W.T. Gordon, E.T. Higgins, W.G. Hind, Swinfen Jordan, A.W.G. Kingsbury, N.F. Large, I.S. Loupekine, C.R. Mapp, J.W.D. Marshall, S.W. Martyn, P.M. Mathews, C.C. Morgan, K. Page, H.G. Pearcey, J.J. Powell, S.H. Reynolds, H. Riley, F. Stenhouse Ross, C.B. Salter, M.J.

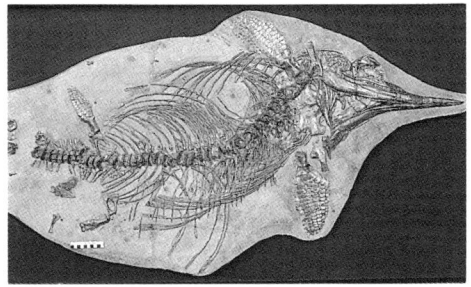

Lower Lias ichthyosaur with embryo from north Somerset coast (BRSMG Ce16611)

Simms, W.W. Stoddart, C.R. Trelease, W.F. Vernon, W.H.V. Wickes and H.H. Winwood.

Major strengths:

Lower Palaeozoic of Tortworth Inlier; Carboniferous Limestone of Avon Gorge and Mendip Hills; Coal Measures of Bristol and Somerset Coalfields; Triassic vertebrates, including *Thecodontosaurus* of Durdham Down; Rhaetic of Aust Cliff; Jurassic of western England, including Lias of Dorset (8m "Charmouth Ichthyosaur" purchased 1988; unique juvenile *Scelidosaurus* dinosaur purchased 1989; ichthyosaur with embryo purchased 1991) and Radstock, Inferior Oolite of Dundry Hill and Cotswolds, Bradford Clay and Kimmeridge Clay of Wiltshire (including 1.8m "Westbury Pliosaur" skull) and Dorset (including most complete ichthyosaur and pycnodont fish known, purchased 1991); Upper Greensand of Blackdown Hills; Pleistocene cave faunas of Durdham Down, Walton and Uphill Bone Caves; minerals of western England, including mendipite and other rare species of Somerset.

Number of specimens:

c. 500,000; c.650 type and figured specimens.

Published catalogues:

Wilson, E. 1890. Fossil types in the Bristol Museum. *Geological Magazine* **7**, 363-372, 411-416.

Crane, M.D. 1980. Catalogue of type, figured and cited fossils in the City of Bristol Museum and Art Gallery, Part 1, Plantae. *Geological Curator* **2** [supplement to part 8, 1-17, i-iv].

Leoffler, E.J. and Crane, M.D. 1982. Catalogue of type, figured and cited fossils in the City of Bristol Museum and Art Gallery, Part 2, Invertebrata: Porifera, Coelenterata, Bryozoa.

Geological Curator **3**, [supplement to part 4, 19-37, v-viii].

Displays:

The geology displays occupy about 250 m² of floor space (first floor rear). *The Changing Earth* was opened in November 1976, tracing the history of the Earth from Precambrian times to the present day, with special reference to the geology of the Bristol area. A new mineral display and a slide-tape show were opened in February 1986. A small *Sea Dragons* gallery and an interactive microcomputer display (Avon geological sites database) both opened 1993.

Public services:

Includes free identification service, access to reference collections by appointment, advice on all aspects of geology (for pupils, students, teachers, planners, landowners, the media), public lectures, etc. Geology Conservation and Advisory Service operated by Section staff and managed by Curator, as an agency service for Area Museum Council for the south-west (from 1989). Advisory and collection survey work undertaken by Curator, laboratory-based conservation by Geology Conservator for AMCSW client museums and others outside the region.

Storage:

In addition to the main geology store (about 185m² and environmentally controlled), there is crated material in a secondary store at the Bristol Industrial Museum.

Research facilities:

Library with British journals, rich in nineteenth-century literature; archives room with manuscript records and indexes; binocular microscopes and other equipment for palaeontological research; equipment for chemical and mechanical preparation, including ultrasonic cleaner, airbrasive unit, air-pens, etc. housed in dedicated Geology Conservation Laboratory (opened 1988) adjacent to main store.

Current projects:

Preparation of *Scelidosaurus* and Kimmeridgian ichthyosaur for display and research. Data collation for catalogue of type, figured and referred specimens. Computerised documentation of the collections. Work on site-recording as part of the National Scheme for Geological Site Documentation and Bristol Regional Environmental Records Centre. Phased upgrade of main store utilising mobile storage units and modern conservation methods.

Staff:

Curators, Peter R. Crowther, MA, AMA, PhD, Roger D. Clark, BSc; Geology Conservator, Roger F. Vaughan, BA, BSc.

Other information:

Other geological resources in close proximity include Bristol Museum Education Service (A. Mathieson) and Bristol Naturalists' Society library in same building; Bristol Environmental Records Centre at Ashton Court Mansion. Bristol University Geology and Extra-mural departments and library in adjoining building.

Compiler:

Peter R. Crowther.

WEST-CENTRAL AND SOUTH-WEST ENGLAND

DEVIZES
Devizes Museum

Address:
41 Long Street, Devizes, SN10 1NS. Telephone 0380 727369.

Administration:
Wiltshire Archaeological and Natural History Society (WANHS).

Admission:
Monday: free. Tuesday - Saturday: adults £1.75; senior citizens, students, parties £1.25; children £0.45.

Times of opening:
Monday - Saturday 10.00 - 17.00.

History:

The WANHS was founded in 1853 with the intent "to foster interest in and to explore the archaeology, antiquities, history, local history and natural history of Wiltshire". The collections were first put on permanent display in 1874 in the building which still forms part of the Museum today. It has since expanded to encompass two houses (both listed buildings), a school hall and an additional extension. The Natural History galleries were opened in 1983 and comprise two sub-divided rooms with the curator's office and stores adjacent.

Principal collections:

The largest is the Society's collection built up since its formation in 1854 by the donations of members and which is still being added to. It contains some exceptionally fine Greensand and Chalk fossils collected by William Cunnington (1813-1906), the majority of whose collection was donated to the British Museum. Other discrete collections include the Luckett Collection, built up by Mr Julian T. Luckett during the late 1960's and early 1970's, and the Rev William Ryton Andrews Collection (1873-1892).

Major strengths:

Palaeontology from the Jurassic and Cretaceous of Wiltshire, especially the Upper Greensand and Chalk.

Number of specimens:

c.6,000; one known type specimen.

Displays:

The Natural History galleries contain panels devoted to the distribution and uses of the Wiltshire rocks, Jurassic and Cretaceous fossils, extinct reptiles and the Pleistocene. Temporary exhibitions are occasionally set up using specimens from the store.

Research facilities:

Binocular microscopes.

Current projects:

Documentation of collection using MODES.

Staff:

Senior Curator, Paul Robinson, PhD, FSA, AMA; Assistant Curator, (Natural Sciences), Andrew Tucker, BSc, MusDip.

Compiler:

Andrew Tucker.

WEST-CENTRAL AND SOUTH-WEST ENGLAND

DORCHESTER
Dorset County Museum

Address:
High West Street, Dorchester, DT1 1XA. Telephone 0305 262735.

Administration:
Dorset Natural History and Archaeological Society.

Admission:
Adults £2.00; senior citizens, children (5-16 years) £1.00; children under 5 free.

Times of opening:
Monday - Saturday 10.00 - 17.00.

History:

The Dorset County Museum from its foundation in 1845 has been based in Dorchester. In 1833 it moved to the present purpose-built home and in 1928 the Museum joined forces with the Dorset Natural History and Antiquarian Field Club to form the Dorset Natural History and Archaeological Society. The Society owns and manages the Dorset County Museum to this day and runs an extensive programme of lectures and events each year.

Major strengths:

Dorset geology, especially fossils from Mesozoic and Caenozoic. An important collection from the Purbeck Limestone Formation includes vertebrate material and dinosaur footprints from Swanage.

Number of specimens:

c.15,000; 20 type, 50 figured, numerous referred specimens.

Publications:

Free leaflets on Dorset Geology and fossils. Proceedings of the DNH&AS published annually.

Displays:

The Geology gallery displays the rocks and fossils of Dorset in stratigraphical order. There are superb ichthyosaur and plesiosaur remains and numerous Jurassic invertebrates. On the main staircase is a massive trunk of a coniferous tree from the Purbeck Beds.

Pliosaur paddle from Kimmeridge Bay

Research facilities:
Binocular microscopes.

Education:
School parties should book with the Education Officer. Fossil workshops available.

Staff:
Deputy Curator, Kate Hebditch.

Compiler:
Kate Hebditch.

WEST-CENTRAL AND SOUTH-WEST ENGLAND

EXETER
Royal Albert Memorial Museum

Address:
Queen Street, Exeter, EX4 3RX. Telephone 0392 265858; Fax 0392 421252.

Administration:
Department of Leisure and Tourism, Exeter City Council.

Admission:
Free, although special summer exhibitions do have a charge.

Times of opening:
Tuesday - Saturday 10.00 - 17.30.

History:

In 1813 the Devon and Exeter Institution (D.& E.I.) attempted to establish a museum in their premises on Cathedral Green, Exeter. This was not a great success due to the limited size of the premises, but these collections formed the nucleus of the Royal Albert Memorial Museum (RAMM) in 1864. At this time work had not begun on the present building and the collections were housed in adjacent rented accommodation until the first phase of the RAMM opened in 1868. The first curator was W.S.M. D'Urban. The collections at this point included large amounts of geological material, probably around 14-15,000 specimens by the turn of the century. The second major phase of development of the collections was under the curatorship of F.R. Rowley between 1902 and 1934.

Principal collections:

Two major periods of collection growth have occurred; the first being from the museum's inception through the curatorship of D'Urban and included those of the D. & E.I., J. Belfield, W. Vicary and many smaller collections. D'Urban himself donated material on a regular basis through the 20th century after he had retired.

The second phase was during the curatorship of F.R. Rowley, curator from 1902-1934. During this period the collections of W.P. Sladen were acquired. These include 3,427 specimens of extant echinoderms, 2,000 fossils, 7,186 microscope slides (including foraminifera collections

of Drs W.B. and P.H. Carpenter) and a library of 2,209 articles. The echinoderms and foraminiferans include material from the voyages of H.M.S. Porcupine and Challenger and contain type and figured material.

Other collections include: Miss J. Linter Collection - recent and fossil mollusca; A. M. Champernowne Collection - over 1,600 fossils and minerals; A.W. Clayden Collection - c.1,600 fossils; Patrick Spencer Collection - vertebrate material (including types) from the Trias between Sidmouth and Budleigh Salterton; C.W. Osman Collection - rock specimens and thin sections (some figured), plus fossils and minerals.

Over recent decades two major acquisitions have been made, namely the Downes Collection of fossils (including types) from the Upper Greensand of Blackdown Hills, and the Spencer Collection of vertebrate fossils from the Triassic of East Devon. The latter has recently been complimented by the donation of an excellent skeleton from these beds by Prof. M. Hart of the University of Plymouth.

Major strengths:

Collections representative of the geology of Devon and its surrounding counties; fossil echinoderms comprising 155 genera and 226 species, largely of asteroids, crinoids and blastoids; Triassic vertebrates from E. Devon; upper Greensand from Haldon Hills and Blackdown Hills.

Number of specimens:

c. 40-50,000 specimens; some type and figured (see above).

Displays:

Geology of Devon - due for replacement; *Sladen Gallery* - display of echinoderms, largely unaltered since 1905 and complemented by Sladen's fine library. The new geology gallery *Geology at Work* opens March 1994.

Staff:

Curator of Natural History, D.E. Bolton.

Compiler:

B.J. Meloy.

WEST-CENTRAL AND SOUTH-WEST ENGLAND

LYME REGIS
Lyme Regis (Philpot) Museum

Address:
Bridge Street, Lyme Regis, DT7 3QA. Telephone 02974 3370.

Administration:
Independent Museum administered by a Trust and run by volunteers. The building is owned and maintained by West Dorset District Council.

Admission:
Adults £0.50; senior citizens £0.40; children £0.25; school parties £0.20.

Times of opening:
Easter (or April 1st) - October: Monday - Saturday 10.30 - 13.00, 14.30 - 17.00, Sunday 14.30 - 17.00.

History:

The Museum was built in 1900-1901 by T.E.D. Philpot, former Mayor of Lyme and great-nephew of the Misses Philpot, important local fossil collectors of the early 19th century. The Museum remained empty until it was given to the Borough in 1920 by his great-niece. The first Curator was Dr Wyatt Wingrave, who exhibited his own collections, and worked closely with Cyril Wanklyn, historian of Lyme. The Museum is built on the site of the birthplace of Mary Anning (1799-1847), another famous local fossil-collector, and geological collections have always figured prominently. It was enhanced and curated during the 1930's by Dr W.D. Lang, Trustee of the Museum, but it languished during and after the war. Efforts were made from the late 1950's to restore order, and culminated in the appointment of John Fowles as Curator in 1978. He published several pamphlets and a book on Lyme's history, enhanced the collections, reorganised the displays and fully recognised the pre-eminence of the geological collection.

Principal collections:

Almost all the collection is local Rhaetian, Jurassic and Cretaceous material from Lyme Regis, Charmouth and their hinterland, mostly fossils, but also some local rocks and sedimentary minerals. Much was collected by Wyatt Wingrave and Lang, the latter's material carries precise source horizon and locality data using his detailed stratigraphy of the local Lower Lias. The Museum has some specimens from the Charmouth collector James Harrison (1819-1864), including the partial leg and other bones of a very young individual of the Lyme Regis dinosaur *Scelidosaurus harrisoni*. The Museum also has some of the surviving core material from the Lyme Regis Borehole of 1901.

Archives:

There is a selection of specimens, books, research papers, documents, paintings and other personal items relating to important 19th century local geologists such as the Anning family, William Buckland, William Conybeare, Henry de la Beche, the Marder family and the Philpot sisters. This rich archive is mostly held by the Dorset County Record Office.

Number of specimens:
6,000.

Publications:
Fowles, J. 1982. *A short history of Lyme Regis.*

Displays:

The present displays include a general display of local fossils, rocks and minerals, and smaller displays devoted to individual geologists and their specimens. A wall display covers the local landslips and their recording by scientists and artists.

Current projects:

Major refurbishment of the building to improve conservation and display of collections in a way worthy of their potential importance.

Education:

Development of educational services is an important part of the above project. A modest start has been made with local primary schools and the new National Curriculum.

Staff:

Hon. Curator, Liz-Anne Bawden.

Other information:

The Museum's position on the sea-front in the heart of town, its charming, idiosyncratic, difficult building, and its connection with Mary Anning and with Lyme as a cradle of palaeontology, gives the collection potential national and international importance. It also benefits from Lyme's outstanding place in literary history from Jane Austin to John Fowles.

Compiler:

Liz-Anne Bawden.

WEST-CENTRAL AND SOUTH-WEST ENGLAND

PLYMOUTH

Plymouth City Museum and Art Gallery

Address:
Drake Circus, Plymouth, PL4 8AJ. Telephone 0752 264878.

Administration:
City of Plymouth Department of Marketing and Leisure.

Admission:
Free.

Times of opening:
Tuesday - Friday 10.00 - 17.30. Saturdays 10.00 - 17.00.

History:

The Museum was founded in 1897 by Plymouth Corporation and opened in temporary premises in 1898 in Beaumont House; it moved to the present purpose built Museum and Art Gallery in 1910. In 1915 it absorbed the collections of Devonport Museum under an Act of Parliament which united the towns of Devonport, Stonehouse and Plymouth. The first curator from 1898-1900 was T.V. Hodgson who served as naturalist with Scott on his first Antarctic Expedition 1901-1904. On his return Hodgson was re-appointed curator from 1907 until his death in 1926. The first Natural History Assistant was appointed in 1955.

Principal collections:

Mainly minerals: Sir John St Aubyn Collection (ex collection William Babington, and 3rd Earl of Bute); Sir William Serjeant Collection (late 19th century, purchased 1924); Rene Gallant Collection (20th century, donated 1986); Richard Barstow Collection (20th century, purchased 1986).

Major strengths:

Minerals from Devon and Cornwall with associated documentation.

Number of specimens:

c. 9,500 minerals, c. 1,600 fossils, c. 900 rocks; no known fossil type material, but majority of St Aubyn Collection comprises referred specimens (Babington 1799).

Published catalogues:

Systematic index to Mineral Collection.

Displays:

Limited geology displays at present. Major re-display of geology planned for 1995 onwards.

Staff:

Keeper of Natural Science, S. Laming, BSc, AMA.

Other information:

Other geological resources in close proximity include University of Plymouth, Department of Geological Sciences.

Compiler:

M.J. Bishop.

WEST-CENTRAL AND SOUTH-WEST ENGLAND

REDRUTH
Camborne School of Mines Geological Museum

Address:
Pool, Redruth, TR15 3SE. Telephone 0209 714866; Fax 0209 716977.

Administration:
Camborne School of Mines, University of Exeter.

Admission:
Free.

Times of opening:
Monday - Friday 09.00 - 17.00. Closed Bank Holidays.

History:

Classes were started for the improvement of Cornish miners at various localities in 1859. By 1887 a Mining School was established at Camborne and similar courses were being run at Redruth and Penzance. Following the death of Robert Hunt, the great innovator of mining education in Cornwall, a memorial museum of minerals and geological specimens was erected in Redruth. The three mining schools were amalgamated in 1909 and became the Camborne School of Metalliferous Mining. An extension to the laboratory in 1891 included a mineralogical museum dedicated to one of the major contributors, G.L. Basset. The Basset Memorial Museum became an important feature of the School with its minerals of interest to mining students. A few specimens were purchased, but most were given. The greater part of the material, containing over one thousand samples, was donated by J.C. Williams of Caerhays Castle. In 1953 the Robert Hunt Collection was transferred to Camborne when the museum building in Redruth was sold. The School moved from the centre of Camborne in 1975 to new premises at Pool. The museum was rehoused in purpose-built accommodation with modern display facilities. In 1993 the School became part of the University of Exeter.

Principal collections:

J.C. Williams (1891); Robert Hunt (1953); F.B. Mitchell (1975); H.A. Thomas (1983); D. Dew (1984); T. Andrews (1985); V. Holyer (1991);

Geology Gallery

R.J. Maunder (1991); E.C.S. Norris (1992); many smaller collections.

Major strengths:

Ores and minerals from UK and abroad; fluorescent and radioactive minerals; Cornish minerals.

Number of specimens:

c.20,000.

Displays:

Gems and ornamental stones; crystals; volcano section with samples; Cornish mining - past and present with 19th century photographic display; radioactive minerals with Geiger counter; sedimentary rocks; fossils illustrating geological time-scale; lode structures; folds and faults; Wheal Jane mine; ores from Franklin Furnace; minerals illustrating short and long wave fluorescence; native elements, sulphides, oxides, sulphates, phosphates, arsenates, vanadates, halides, carbonates and silicates - displays of minerals classified according to crystal chemistry; rock suites from various localities around the world; classification of rocks; aids to mineral identification includes colour, streak, hardness, twinning, etc.); Cornish minerals.

Research facilities:

Access to the following may be arranged: research microscopes with photographic facilities; specimen photography, also a range of photographic equipment including dark rooms; rock splitting, sawing, grinding, polishing facilities; thin and polished sections; X-ray diffraction and X-ray fluorescence, scanning electron microscopy and chemical techniques for identification. A wide range of computer facilities is available and the School has an excellent library with photocopying services.

Current projects:

Computerisation of catalogues is in progress. Cornish gallery partially complete, new shop recently opened.

Staff:

Curator, R.L. Atkinson, PhD.

Other information:

Other geological resources in close proximity include the Geology Department of Camborne School of Mines and Truro Museum.

Compiler:

R.L. Atkinson.

WEST-CENTRAL AND SOUTH-WEST ENGLAND

TAUNTON
Somerset County Museum

Address:
Taunton Castle, Castle Green, Taunton, TA1 4AA.
Telephone 0823 255504/325762.

Administration:
Somerset County Council Museums Service.

Admission:
Adults (over 18) £1.50; senior citizens £1.00; children (over 5), students (on production of Student card), disabled and the unemployed £0.40; children under 5, and members of affiliated organisations free.[Affiliated organisations: Somerset Archaeological and Natural History Society, Museums Association, Friends of the Abbey Barn and Taunton Castle and members of subscribing educational institutions.]

Times of opening:
Monday - Saturday 10.00 - 17.00. Closed Christmas Day, Boxing Day, New Year's Day and Good Friday.

History:

The collections now in the care of the Somerset County Museums Service were started in 1849 with the founding of the Somerset Archaeological and Natural History Society (SANHS). The Society's secretary, the Rev. T.F. Dymock, speaking in 1849 was very keen that "...no time be lost in getting together a collection of sufficient importance to be of real help to those studies which the Society is established to promote", i.e. archaeology, history and the natural sciences of Somersetshire (Dymock 1851, p. 7). The Society's headquarters and museum were established in the county town of Taunton in 1850 in a rented room.

In 1873 the Society took possession of Taunton Castle. Part of the building was to be occupied by the Society's offices and part by its museum and rapidly expanding collections. New extensions were added to the castle in the 1930's as space had become limited, due in no small way to the collecting of H. St George Gray, curator from 1901 to 1949.

As a result of the growing costs the Society turned to the local authority (Somerset County Council) for assistance which initially came in the form of an annual grant. In 1958 the castle was placed with the county council on a 49 year lease which included responsibility for maintaining the building. The collections were leased to the council for the same period on the understanding that full care be provided. The Society maintains close links and its offices and library are still housed in the castle.

Principal collections:

Spencer George Perceval Collection (1852-1863) - west Somerset minerals from Brendon and Quantock Hills; Lyme Borehole Collection (1901); Puriton Borehole Collection (1909-1910); C.H. Fox Collection - Upper Greensand invertebrates (mainly molluscs) from the Blackdown Hills; D. Williams Collection - Devonian, Carboniferous, Jurassic and Cretaceous of Cornwall, Devon and Somerset, plus much Pleistocene bones from the Mendips; W. Beard Collection - Pleistocene mammals; E. Bower Collection - Jurassic and Cretaceous invertebrates of Yeovil; H.F. Parsons Collection - Jurassic invertebrates of Frome; C. Tomkins Collection - Jurassic invertebrates (mainly molluscs) from Wiltshire and Somerset, plus silicified Portland plants from Dorset and Carboniferous echinoderms from the Mendips; Canon R.J. Meade Collection - Jurassic invertebrates of Warminster and Castle Cary; Rev. J.G. Howe Collection - mainly molluscs from the Red Crag; C. Moore Collection - Jurassic molluscs from Wiltshire, Somerset and Calvados, France, possibly including many status specimens.

Major strengths:

Fossils and minerals from Somerset and neighbouring areas, especially Pleistocene vertebrates, Devonian and Carboniferous invertebrates, Jurassic and Cretaceous invertebrates, west Somerset minerals, Somerset vertebrates, plants from the Somerset Coalfield, insects from the Upper Lias of Ilminster.

Number of specimens:

c.20,000; 8 type, 2 figured, 1 referred, plus many undocumented status specimens from the Quaternary mammal bone collections and possibly others from the Moore Collection.

Displays:

The geology gallery created by A. Hallam was dismantled in 1978 and has not been replaced. The present display consists entirely of Hallam's work transported to a temporary location. A new display is planned, but exhibition space is small (40m^2).

Staff:

Keeper of Natural Sciences, Dennis W. Parsons.

Compiler:

Dennis Parsons.

WEST-CENTRAL AND SOUTH-WEST ENGLAND

TORQUAY
Torquay Museum

Address:
529 Babbacombe Road, Torquay, TQ1 1HG.
Telephone 0803 293975.

Administration:
Torquay Natural History Society.

Admission:
Adults £1.75; senior citizens, children £1.00; pre-booked groups £0.75 each with free entry for leader; junior school groups £0.50.

Times of opening:
Monday - Friday 10.00 - 16.45. (also Saturday between Easter and October). Sunday 13.30 - 16.45.

History:

The Torquay Natural History Society was founded in 1844. Its original intention was to collect books and later specimens relating to natural history, but other unrelated items also found their way into the stores. In 1875 the Society established its own purpose built museum, which has subsequently undergone enlargement. The displays cover geology, palaeontology and wildlife of Devon, paintings, prints and photographs of South Devon and Torbay, archaeological finds in particular from Kent's cavern and Victoriana.

Principal collections:

Minerals: Admiral Bedford; Dr J.P. Way. Rocks: Hansford-Worth; Milton; Dr F. Krantz; S. Henson; US National Museum; Admiral Bedford; W.A.E. Ussher; A. Somervail; R.N. Worth; L. Jackson; I. Rogers; Lee; A.R. Hunt; Fox and Hinde; W.J. Else. Fossils: A.J. Jukes-Brown (1914); Beattle (1927); J.G. Hamling; Dr Battersby; Llewelen; Bearcroft.

Major strengths:

Devonian material.

Number of specimens:

10,860 rocks, 5,160 minerals, 3,500 fossils.

Published catalogues:

Jukes-Brown, A.J. & Else, W.J. 1907. A list of the type fossils and figured specimens in the museum of the Torquay Natural History Society. *Transactions of the Devonshire Association* **39**, 399-409.

Displays:

400,000,000 years in Devon, which includes fossils from the Devonian, Carboniferous and Mesozoic, rocks from the Tertiary, stalagmites and stalactites, minerals and mining, plus pictorial and diagrammatic displays on Tors, China Clay and granite.

Research facilities:

Petrological microscope.

Current projects:

Cataloguing of mineral collection.

Staff:

Curator, Ann Inscker, BSc, MPhil, PIFA; Assistant Curator, Barry Chander, BA.

Other information:

Other geological resources in close proximity include Kent's Cavern.

Compiler:

A. Inscker.

WEST-CENTRAL AND SOUTH-WEST ENGLAND

TRURO
Royal Cornwall Museum

Address:
River Street, Truro, TR1 2SJ. Telephone 0872 72205.

Administration:
Royal Institution of Cornwall.

Admission:
Adults £1.00; senior citizens, unaccompanied children £0.50; accompanied children and school parties free.

Times of opening:
Monday - Saturday 09.00 - 17.00. Closed Bank Holidays, Good Friday, Christmas Eve, Christmas Day, Boxing Day.

History:

A Literary and Philosophical Society for the Advancement of Cornish History and Science was the forerunner of the Royal Institution of Cornwall which was founded in 1818 and established a museum almost immediately. The Museum moved to its present site during the First World War and was opened in 1919. The front part of the building had been a bank, and for some time a mining school, but the galleries behind were purpose-built as a museum.

Principal collections:

Philip Rashleigh (1729-1811) of Menabilly near Fowey; James Wickett (1841-1921) of Redruth.

Archives:

Large collection of negatives and photographs of Cornwall which include glass plate negatives of underground mining scenes taken by J.C. Burrow (1852-1914) of Camborne between 1892 and 1910.

Major strengths:

Cornish rocks and fossils, but mainly Cornish minerals. The most important mineral collection is that of Philip Rashleigh who began collecting in 1760 and exchanged minerals throughout Britain and Europe; the collection houses classic specimens from Banat (Romania), Germany and Russia, as well as from the north of England, the Isle of Man etc. This collection also contains an unrivalled suite of secondary coppers from the Gwennap mines, notably from Wheal Gorland and adjoining setts. Wickett's

Botryoidal chalcopyrite from Redruth area

collection includes a world-wide suite of cassiterites.

Number of specimens:

c.20,000; many figured minerals from Rashleigh's catalogue (see below) and from J. Sowerby's *British mineralogy* (1804-17).

Published catalogues:

Rashleigh, P. 1797, 1802. *Specimens of British minerals selected from the cabinet of Philip Rashleigh, vols 1 & 2.* W. Bulmer & Co., London.

Displays:

The Rashleigh Gallery has been completely refurbished and was re-opened to the public at the end of March 1993. It displays not only minerals but models of mine pumping engines and gives a brief history of Cornish mining from the Early Bronze Age to the present day, including the relatively recent china clay industry. Related industries, including tin smelting and cooperage are also included.

Current projects:

Former Baptists Church now linked to the museum and open as a cafe, art gallery and lecture hall. New store recently completed behind the former church.

Staff:

Senior Curator, R.D. Penhallurick.

Compiler:

R.D. Penhallurick.

WEST-CENTRAL AND SOUTH-WEST ENGLAND

WELLS

Wells Museum

Address:
8 Cathedral Green, Wells, BA5 2UE. Telephone 0749 673477.

Administration:
Trustees and Managers of Wells Museum. Collection management - Somerset County Museum Service.

Admission:
Adults £1.00; senior citizens, children, students (on production of Student card) £0.50.

Times of opening:
Easter - 31 October: Monday - Saturday 10.00 -17.30, Sunday 11.00 - 17.30; 1 November - Easter: Wednesday - Sunday 11.00 - 16.00.

History:
Founded 1893 by H.E. Balch, noted local archaeologist and one of the earliest cavers in the Mendips. Collections originally housed in one room above the west cloister of Wells Cathedral. In 1928 William Wyndham purchased the present building and presented it for the purpose of providing a public museum. The Wells museum moved into these premises in 1932. The museum is an independent charitable trust, run by a group of Trustees and Managers. H.E. Balch was honorary curator from 1893 until 1954, succeeded by a number of honorary curators until 1987. During 1987 the Trustees and Managers entered into a management agreement with Somerset County Council Museums Service.

Principal collections:
Thomas Willcox Collection - local minerals.

Major strengths:
Local minerals; Jurassic fossils; Palaeozoic fossils; local Pleistocene from Badger Hole and Milton Hill.

Number of specimens:
c.4,300.

Displays:
Geological displays cover local minerals, non-metallic and metallic minerals and fossils from the Palaeozoic, Jurassic and Pleistocene. Balch Room displays Pleistocene material from Badger Hill and Milton Hill.

Staff:
Curator, Lesley-Anne Kerr.

Compiler:
Dennis Parsons.

WEST-CENTRAL AND SOUTH-WEST ENGLAND

WESTON-SUPER-MARE
Woodspring Museum

Address:
Burlington Street, Weston-super-Mare, BS23 1PR. Telephone 0934 621028; Fax 0934 612006.

Administration:
Woodspring District Council Department of Leisure.

Admission:
Adults £1.60; senior citizens, children £0.80; family ticket (2 adults, 3 children) £3.60.

Times of opening:
Tuesday - Sunday 10.00 - 17.00.

History:

Journeyman Cordwainer William Mable began collecting antiquities in the Weston-super-Mare area in the early 1850's. In 1861 he made his collections available to the public primarily for their education in the Albert Memorial Museum and Industrial School, behind Emmanuel Church, Weston. In 1901 the trustees gave the collections to the people of Weston, and the Borough constructed a custom-built building to house the town's Library and Museum. In 1974 Weston Borough was subsumed within the new District of Woodspring which took over the running of the museum. In 1975 Woodspring Museum moved to its present premises, previously the Weston Gaslight Company's stores and workshop.

Major strengths:

Mendip minerals.

Number of specimens:

1,300 minerals, 1,000 fossils, some rocks; one type specimen (an ichthyosaur forefin from the holotype in the Natural History Museum).

Displays:

The only pure geological displays deal with mineralisation and include many Mendip specimens. The new natural history gallery includes some Mendip minerals and rocks.

Staff:

Natural History Officer, Nick Goff.

Compiler:

N. Goff.

CHANNEL ISLANDS
GUERNSEY
Guernsey Museum and Art Gallery

Address:
Candie Gardens, St Peter Port, Guernsey. Telephone 0481 726518; Fax 0481 715177; Natural History Officer 0481 720513; Fax 0481 728671.

Administration:
In essence a national museum service, directly funded by the States of Guernsey, administered by the States of Guernsey Heritage Committee and staffed by Guernsey Civil Servants.

Admission:
Adults £2.00; senior citizens £1.00; children £0.75; family group £4.50. Joint tickets (to include entry into other Guernsey museums) and season tickets (to include unlimited entry) also available at advantageous rates.

Times of opening:
Daily 10.30 - 17.30 (winter closing 16.30). Closed Christmas.

History:

The States of Guernsey first became involved with museums in 1907, when the Lukis family archaeological and natural history collections were left to the Island. Part of the Lukis family residence was subsequently opened as a museum. In the 1930's the museum was moved, re-opening as the Lukis & Island Museum in a deconsecrated church. This closed to the public in 1970, due to structural problems with the building. In 1973 the first full-time professional curator was appointed, to oversee development which culminated in 1978 with the opening of Guernsey Museum and Art Gallery. In 1978 the service also assumed responsibility for the collections from an earlier independent museum attached to the Guille-Allès Library.

Principal collections:

Lukis Collection - initiated by Frederick Corbin Lukis (1788-1871) and added to by friends and children, notably John Walter Lukis (1816-1894) - mainly local and European minerals (c.3,000 specimens) and fossils (c.1,500 specimens); Guille-Allès Museum Collection - includes collections from the Guernsey Mechanics Institution (founded 1831), plus the personal collections of the founders of the Guille-Allès

Library, Thomas Guille (1817-1896) and Frederick Mansell Allès (1818-1895), which include much American material; plus a collection of minerals given by the widow of Gilbert Hamilton (1803-1882); Zachary Robert Collection - petrological specimens (>1,000) including many from Channel Islands.

Archives:

F.C. Lukis manuscript catalogue of minerals still exists.

Number of specimens:

c.7,000.

Publications:

Roach, R.A. et al. 1991. Outline and guide to the geology of Guernsey. *Guernsey Museum Monographs*, **3**.

Anon. *The Geology of Guernsey*. Guernsey Museum Information Sheet.

Displays:

Sequence of permanent displays on the geological and natural environment of Guernsey, and continuing with the human history of the island. The programme of temporary exhibitions occasionally has some geological content.

Public services:

The museum offers a full public and academic enquiry service. The collections, archives and library holdings of the museum are available for examination by appointment. Loans for scientific study would be subject to curatorial approval.

Research facilities:

Binocular microscope, and small departmental

library with general and Guernsey related natural history and geological material.

Current projects:

Improving collection documentation using MDA MODES software. There are plans to move the Natural History collections to a self contained storage unit, with office accommodation and technical facilities. The section is currently seeking to extend its role in environmental recording for the island.

Education:

Educational use of the collections is normally arranged through the Museum Education Officer.

Staff:

Keeper of Natural History, A.C. Howell, MSc, FMA.

Compiler:

A.C. Howell.

CHANNEL ISLANDS

JERSEY
La Hougue Bie Museum

Address:
Grouville, Jersey. Telephone 0534 853823 Fax 0534 66085.

Administration:
La Hougue Bie Museum is part of the Jersey Museums Service, and is operated by the Jersey Heritage Trust, an independent body which includes representatives of the States of Jersey and the Société Jersiaise. The collections are the property of the latter.

Admission:
Adults £2.00; children, students, senior citizens £1.00. Groups receive 25% discount booked in advance.

Times of opening:
March - October: Daily 10.00 - 17.00. (Parties should be booked in advance through the Operations Manager at the Jersey Museum, The Weighbridge, St Helier.)

History:

The Société Jersiaise was formed in 1873 for the study of the history, language, geology, natural history and antiquities of Jersey. At an early stage the collections included geological specimens, which were initially displayed at the Society's museum at St Helier, but which were moved to a purpose built geology gallery at La Hougue Bie, Grouville in 1979. The Jersey Museums Service was established in 1985 and provides professional curatorial and display facilities for the Société's collections.

Principal collections:
Société Jersiaise (1873-present).

Major strengths:
The museum concentrates essentially on the geology of Jersey, but also has a small comparative collection. Strengths include: Brioverian shales; intrusive and extrusive igneous formations; mineralogy of Jersey; conglomerates; Quaternary geology; geology of Les Ecrehous & Les Minquiers.

Number of specimens:
3,000.

The largest known spherulite from the rhyolite at Bouley Bay, 20" x 18"

Displays:
The M.P. Shah Geology Gallery has displays devoted to the mineralogy of Jersey, the Brioverian shale series, the Jersey volcanic series, the Rozel conglomerates, the geology of Les Minquiers and Les Ecrehous and the Quaternary geology of Jersey.

Research facilities:
The Geology Section of the Société Jersiaise have binocular and petrological microscopes and rock cutting facilities.

Education:
The Jersey Museums Service employs an Education Officer who can be contacted at the Jersey Museum.

Staff:
Curator of Archaeology, Olga Finch, BA.

Compiler:
M. Patton.

Appendix

Almond Valley Heritage Centre,
Millfield, Kirkton North, Livingston, EH54 7AR. Tel. 0506 414957.

Arbroath Museum,
Signal Tower, Ladyloan, Arbroath, DD11 1PU. Tel. 0241 75598.

Arbuthnot Museum,
St Peter's Street, Peterhead, AB42 6QD. Tel. 0779 77778.

Armagh County Museum,
The Mall East, Armagh, BT61 9BE. Tel. 0861 523070.

Auld Kirk Museum,
Cowgate, Kirkintilloch, G66 1AB. tel. 041 775 1185.

Banff Museum,
High Street, Banff. Tel. 0799 77778.

Bankfield Museum,
Boothtown Road, Halifax, HX3 6HG. Tel. 0422 352334.

Bath Geology Museum,
18 Queen Square, Bath, BA1 2HP. Tel. 0225 28144.

Bo'ness Heritage Trust,
62 Union Street, Bo'ness, EH51 9AH. Tel. 0506 825855.

Borough of Darlington Museum,
Tubwell Row, Darlington, DL1 1PD. Tel. 0325 463795.

Botanic Gardens Museum,
Botanic Gardens, Botanic Road, Churchtown, Southport, PR9 7NB.

Bournemouth Museums Service,
Russell-Cotes Art Gallery and Museum, East Cliff, Bournemouth, BH1 3AA. Tel. 0202 551009.

Bournemouth Natural Science Society,
Museum and Library, 39 Church Road, Bournemouth, BH1 3NS. Tel. 0202 23525.

Brander Museum,
The Square, Huntly, Aberdeenshire, Tel. 0779 77778.

Brecknock Museum,
Captains Walk, Brecon, LD3 7DW. Tel.0874 624121.

Buteshire Natural History Museum,
Stuart Street, Rothesay, PA20 0BR.

Campbeltown Public Library and Museum,
Hall Street, Campbeltown, PA28 6BJ. Tel. 0586 52366.

Carmarthen Museum,
Quay Street, Abergwili, Carmarthen, SA13 2JG. Tel. 0267 231691.

Carnegie Museum,
The Square, Inverurie. Tel. 0779 77778.

Central Museum,
Victoria Avenue, Southend-on-sea, SS2 6EW. Tel. 0702 330214.

Chelmsford and Essex Museum,
Oaklands Park, Moulsham Street, Chelmsford, CM2 9AQ. Tel. 0245 353066.

Chichester District Museum,
29 Little London, Chichester, PO19 1PB. Tel. 0243 784638.

Clun Local History Museum,
Town Hall, Clun, SW7 8JU. Tel. 05884 576.

Creetown Gem Rock Museum and Crystal Cave,
Chain Road, Creetown, DG8 7HT. Tel. 067182 357.

Dick Institute Museum,
Elmbank Avenue, Kilmarnock, KA1 3BU. Tel.0563 26401.

Dinosaurland,
Combe Street, Lyme Regis, DT7 3NY. Tel. 02974 3541.

Dorman Memorial Museum,
Linthorpe Road, Middlesborough, TS6 6LA. Tel. 0642 813781.

Dunfermline District Museum,
Viewfield Terrace, Dunfermline, KY12 7HY. Tel. 0383 721814.

East Kent Geological Site Record Centre,
City Museums, High Street, Canterbury, CT1 2JE.

Elgin Museum,
1 High Street, Elgin, IV30 1EQ. Tel. 0343 543675.

Falconer Museum,
Tolbooth Street, Forres, IV36 0PH. Tel. 0309 73701.

Forest of Dean,
Royal Forest of Dean Centre for Environmental Studies, Mitcheldean, GL17 0AH. Tel. 0594 542551.

Glencoe and North Lorn Museum,
Glencoe Village, Glencoe. Tel. 08552 332.

Gloucester City Museum and Art Gallery,
Brunswick Road, Gloucester, GL1 1HP. Tel. 0452 524131.

Gunnersby Park Museum,
Gunnersbury Park, London, W3 8LQ. Tel. 081 992 1612.

Hartlepool Museum Service,
Gray Museum and Art Gallery, Clarence Road, Hartlepool, TS24 8BT. Tel. 0429 266522, ext. 2610.

Hastings Museum and Art Gallery,
Cambridge Road, Hastings, TN34 1ET. Tel. 0424 721202.

Hawick Museum and the Scott Gallery,
Wilton Lodge, Hawick, TD9 7JL. Tel. 0450 73457.

Herbert Art Gallery and Museum,
Jordan Well, Coventry, CV1 5RW. Tel. 0203 832375.

Hugh Miller's Cottage,
Church Street, Cromarty, IV11 8XA. Tel. 03817 245.

Ilfracombe Museum,
Wilder Road, Ilfracombe, EX43 8AF. Tel. 0271 63541.

Inverness Museum and Art Gallery,
Castle Wynd, Inverness, IV2 3ED. Tel. 0463 237112.

Isles of Scilly Museum,
Church Street, St Mary's, Isles of Scilly, TR21 0JJ. Tel. 0720 22337.

Keswick Education Service,
Blencathra Centre, Threlkeld, Keswick, CA12 4SG. Tel. 07687 79601.

Kirkcaldy Museums and Art Gallery,
War Memorial Gardens, Kirkcaldy, KY1 1YG. Tel. 0592 260732.

Kyle and Carrick District Libraries and Museums Service.
Carnegie Library, 12 Main Street, Ayr, KA8 8ED. Tel. 0292 269141, ext. 5227.

Laing Museum,
High Street, Newburgh, KY14 6DX. Tel. 0334 53722, ext. 141.

Lead Mining Museum,
Goldscaur Row, Wanlockhead, ML12 6UT. Tel. 0659 74387.

London Borough of Bromley Museum,
The Priory, Churchill, Orpington, BR6 0HH. Tel. 0689 873826.

Lound Hall Mining Museum,
Lound Hall, Bothamsall, Retford. Tel. 0623 860728.

Luton Museum,
Wardown Park, Luton, LU2 7HA. Tel. 0582 36941/2.

Maidstone Museum and Art Gallery,
St Faiths Street, Maidstone, ME14 1LH. Tel. 0622 754497.

Manx National Heritage,
Crellins Hill, Douglas, Isle of Man. tel. 0624 675522.

McLean Museum and Art Gallery,
15 Kelly Street, Greenock, PA16 8JX. Tel. 0475 23741.

Newbury District Museum,
The Wharf, Newbury, RG14 5AS. Tel. 0635 30511.

Norris Library and Museum,
The Broadway, St Ives, PE17 4BX. Tel. 0480 65101.

North East Fife District Museum Service,
County Buildings, Cupar, KY15 4TA. Tel. 0334 53722, ext. 141.

Oxfordshire County Museum Fletcher's House,
Woodstock, Oxford, OX20 1SN. Tel. 0993 811456.

Paisley Museum and Art Galleries,
High Street, Paisley, PA1 2BA. Tel. 041 889 3151.

Peak District Mining Museum,
The Pavilion, Matlock Bath, DE4 3PS. Tel. 0629 583834.

Penrith Museum,
Robinson's School, Middlegate, Penrith, CA11 7PT. Tel. 0768 64671, ext. 288.

Rotherham Museum and Art Gallery,
Clifton Park, Rotherham, S65 1JH. Tel. 0709 382121.

Rozelle House Museum,
Monument Road, Alloway, Ayr, KA7 4NQ. Tel. 0292 45447.

Ruskin Museum,
The Institute, Yewdale Road, Coniston, LA21 8EH. Tel. 05394 41387.

Saint Helens Museum and Art Gallery,
College Street, St Helens, WA10 1TW. Tel. 0744 24061/2960.

Scottish Mining Museum,
Lady Victoria Colliery, Newtongrange, EH22 4QN. Tel. 031 663 7519.

Skye Environmental Centre Ltd.,
Broadford, Isle of Skye, IV49 9AQ.

Spalding Gentleman's Society Museum,
9 Broad Street, Spalding, PE11 1TB. Tel. 0775 724658.

Stevenage Museum,
St George's Way, Stevenage, SG1 1XX. Tel. 0438 354292.

Stewartry Museum,
St Mary Street, Kirkcudbright, DG6 4QA. Tel. 0557 31643.

Stirling Smith Art Gallery and Museum,
40 Albert Place, Dumbarton Road, Stirling, FK8 2RQ. Tel. 0786 71917.

Stockport Museum,
Vernon Park, Turncroft Lane, Offerton, Stockport, SK1 4AR. Tel. 061 474 4460.

Stromness Museum,
52 Alfred Street, Stromness, KW16 3DF. Tel. 0856 850025.

Swindon Museum and Art Gallery,
Bath Road, Swindon. Tel. 0793 493188.

Swiss Cottage Museum,
Osborne House, East Cowes, PO32 6JY. Tel. 0983 292511.

Thurso Heritage Society,
High Street, Thurso.

Tiverton Museum,
St Andrew Street, Tiverton, EX16 6PH. Tel. 0884 256295.

Totnes Museum,
70 Fore Street, Totnes, TQ9 5RU. Tel. 0803 863821.

Tunbridge Wells Museum,
Civic Centre, Mount Pleasant, Royal Tunbridge Wells, TN1 1RS. Tel. 0892 526121, ext. 3171.

Tweeddale Museum,
Chambers Institute, High Street, Peebles, EH45 8AP. Tel. 0721 20123.

Water Power Museum,
Finch Foundry, Sticklepath, Okehampton, EX20 2NW. Tel. 0837 840104.

Wigtown District Museum,
The Old Town Hall, 55 George Street, Stranraer, DG9 7JP. Tel. 0776 5088.

Worthing Museum and Art Gallery,
Chapel Road, Worthing, BN11 1HP. Tel. 0903 239999, ext. 2528.